MARCEL: The Right Hand of God

THE REMNANT

FADE IN: The following quote ~~~  it
the present time there is a r
grace and truth"

- Romans 11:05

FADE IN:

THE MOTU PROPRIO

FADE IN: The date July, 17 2007 appears on the screen.

EXT. - DAY - ST PETERS SQUARE

Pope Benedict XVI is seen delivering his decree the Motu Proprio reinstating the Latin Mass as the Extraordinary Mass of the Church.

              CUT TO:

         VATICAN REPORTER
    We are hear today in Rome where
    Pope Benedict, a former Hitler
    youth, will tell Roman Catholic
    priests in coming days that they
    can say mass in Latin a dead
    language the no one knows anymore
    as a concession to right wing
    extremists in the church, known as
    traditionalists. We are here with a
    a Roman Catholic priest to gain
    further insight into this Motu
    Proprio. Fr. Swartz can you explain
    this to us?

         FR. SWARTZ
    The decree by the Pope is known as
    a Motu Proprio. This cryptic latin
    phrase can be loosely translated *"I
    can do whatever I want because I am
    the Pope and you can't stop me."*

         VATICAN REPORTER
    Why would the Pope issue such a
    decree?

              (CONTINUED)

MARCEL: The Right Hand of God
CONTINUED:

>   FR. SWARTZ
>   The Latin Mass, also known as the
>   Tridentine mass, is a product of
>   the 'dark ages' and was
>   understandably jettisoned by the
>   reforms of the Second Vatican
>   Council in the 1960's. The latin
>   mass is said by the priest with his
>   back to the congregation whispering
>   secret prayers that only he can
>   understand. In the Tridentine mass
>   the laity does not participate at
>   all , so they often turn to
>   knitting, macramé, or checkers to
>   pass the time.
>
>   VATICAN REPORTER
>   How ridiculous.
>
>   FR. SWARTZ
>   The move by the Pope has raised
>   concern about reviving parts of the
>   old liturgy that Jews consider anti-
>   Semitic, gays consider homo-phobic,
>   women consider sexist, dwarves
>   consider anti-dwarfic (communion
>   rails are too high), and priests
>   consider too difficult to learn.
>
>   VATICAN REPORTER
>   The publication of this document is
>   to be accompanied by a letter from
>   the Pope, a former Hitler youth, to
>   individual bishops explaining why
>   he is doing this against their will
>   and better judgment. Is that true?
>
>   FR. SWARTZ
>   We priests, Bishops and even
>   Cardinals are very disturbed by
>   this action by the Pope. We are
>   very, very upset about this. It is
>   widely believed that the Pope is
>   restoring the mass as a cop out to
>   the right wing group known as
>   Lefebvrists and that this
>   constitutes a complete rejection of
>   all the reforms of Vatican II.

(CONTINUED)

MARCEL: The Right Hand of God
CONTINUED:

>   VATICAN REPORTER
>   What do you see as the Pope's next
>   steps?
>
>   FR. SWARTZ
>   It remains unclear at this time,
>   since the exact contents of the
>   documents are still unknown.
>
>   VATICAN REPORTER
>   How long will it be before the
>   Church sets up the Inquisition
>   again?
>
>   FR. SWARTZ
>   Who knows what to expect from a
>   Pope who just turned the Church
>   back 50 years. But, details should
>   be available in a few days.

THE INTRODUCTION OF FR. GABRIELLI AND FR. JAEGER

EXT. - DAY - ST PETERS SQUARE

Two Priests Fr. Michael Gabrielli (Age 85) a retired Holy
Ghost Priest and Fr. Walter Jaeger (Age 32) a diocesan priest
from Chicago start walking away from St. Peters Square and
are heading towards an outside cafe. It is a sunny day and
the streets are heavily crowded. As Fr. Gabrielli signals a
waiter for a table, the discussion begins.

>   FR. MICHAEL GABRIELLI
>   Fr. Jaeger if you only knew the
>   long road that got us here today.
>
>   FR. WALTER JAEGER
>   Road? Which road?
>
>   FR. MICHAEL GABRIELLI
>   The road of Archbishop Lefebvre.
>   The Traditionalist movement.

As Fr. Gabrielli finishes his statements he notices a priest
walking across the street that looks like the s/he devil
character that was used in the Passion of Christ. The figure
gives Fr.

(CONTINUED)

MARCEL: The Right Hand of God
   CONTINUED:

Gabrielli a stern look and then a sickly smile before disappearing into an alley. Fr. Gabrielli looks back at Fr. Jaeger.

> FR. WALTER JAEGER
> Father, I would never had thought the Pope would ever reinstitute the old mass. Wasn't he responsible for the excommunications of Archbishop Lefebvre?

> FR. MICHAEL GABRIELLI
> Well he was the one who was interceding on behalf of Pope John Paul II at that time since he was the Secretary of State at that time.

> FR. WALTER JAEGER
> So would you say this Motu Proprio was the result of Archbishop Lefebvre's efforts?

> FR. MICHAEL GABRIELLI
> Of Course! To think our Church would be turned upside down in the 1960's and 1970's and now it maybe turning back to its glorious days.

> FR. WALTER JAEGER
> All because of Archbishop Lefebvre?

> FR. MICHAEL GABRIELLI
> Yes because there was no one else and to think it all came about due to a simple boy from France.

                                        FADE OUT.

   FADE IN:

MEET THE LEFEBVRE'S

MARCEL: The Right Hand of God

INT. - DAY - TOURCOING NORD, FRANCE - ST JEAN-BAPTISTE CATHOLIC CHURCH - WINTER 1914

This is where the name of the movie first appears on the screen in old english script: 𝔐𝔞𝔯𝔠𝔢𝔩: 𝔗𝔥𝔢 ℜ𝔦𝔤𝔥𝔱 ℌ𝔞𝔫𝔡 𝔬𝔣 𝔊𝔬𝔡 a Gregorian Chant will start that will lead into the opening scene of the Lefebvre Family attending morning mass. The Church is full and a low Latin Mass is being said. The scene jumps to the entire Lefebvre family at the communion rail receiving communion all lined up next to each other. Marcel Lefebvre is looking up at his father kneeing next to him with great admiration. The next scene is the family all leaving church together. Mrs Lefebvre (Gabrielle) heads away towards their home with the two youngest children as the other all run ahead of Marcel and Rene Sr. Rene Sr is holding Marcels hand very tightly. As Marcel looks around he spots a factory worker that is the same s/he devil figure. The look of the factory worker is pure evil and it causes Marcel to look away and hold his father's hand even tighter. At the same time factory workers and neighbors exchange pleasantries as they pass. One of the factory workers stops to address Rene Sr.

          JOSEPH - MALE FACTORY WORKER
Mr. Lefebrve my wife is about to deliver our 6th child and I may need to leave early today in case she goes into labor. Is that okay with you?

          RENE LEFEBRVE SR
Joseph there are only two greater authorities in my factory than me. One is God and the others are all my workers wives (laughing as he says wives). (In a serious voice) Of course your first responsibility is your family. I hope all goes well and let me know if there is anything we can do for your family.

          JOSEPH - MALE FACTORY WORKER
Thank you Mr. Lefebrve! (Joseph hurries away out of fear that Rene may change his mind)

          RENE LEFEBRVE SR
(yelling out to Joseph since he is hurrying away) Joseph whether your child is a boy or girl - Rene is a wonderful name (laughing)

(CONTINUED)

MARCEL: The Right Hand of God
CONTINUED:

A wagon of soldiers heading past Rene Sr and Marcel cause then to stop and let it pass. The soldiers have a scared look on their faces. At the same time a soldier with one leg missing on one crutch is heading in the opposite direction. Once again Marcel squeezes his fathers hand.

                    RENE LEFEBRVE SR (CONT'D)
        Marcel this war is like no other.
        This is the first time that the
        entire world seems to be involved.

                    MARCEL LEFEBVRE
        Father why are we at war? What have
        we done?

                    RENE LEFEBRVE SR
        Marcel it is not what anyone person
        has done wrong. War is the surest
        sign that the devil truly exists
        amongst us. But you need not worry
        about the war you need to worry
        about your schooling now. So lets
        get you there before Sister Cecilia
        Marie yells at me again.

                    MARCEL LEFEBVRE
        Me too!

As Marcel enters the school (academy) with a nun following up behind him ushering him into the doors, a man approaches Rene Sr. to have a discussion. Rene Sr. Waits until the school door closes before he acknowledges the man approaching.

                    BRITISH INTELLIGENCE OFFICER
        Rene we have to talk! (as he looks
        around suspiciously to see if
        anyone is watching)

                    RENE LEFEBRVE SR
        Lets move to my factory office.

As they both walk through the factory, all the workers are greeting Rene Sr. as he passes. They begin to ascend a stair case to an upper level of the factory towards Rene's office. The British Intelligence officer begins to talk to Rene Sr.

                    BRITISH INTELLIGENCE OFFICER
        The word has reach our office that
        you have been identified as the
        intelligence officer of Tourcoing-
        Nord.
                (MORE)

                                              (CONTINUED)

MARCEL: The Right Hand of God
CONTINUED:

> **BRITISH INTELLIGENCE OFFICER (CONT'D)**
> The Germans know you have been helping French and British prisoners escape from behind enemy lines. It won't be long before they come for you.

They arrive at Rene's office and he waits to respond until he gets into his office and then closes the door tightly behind him.

> **RENE LEFEBRVE SR**
> It was just a matter of time. We knew they would eventually find out from someone.

> **BRITISH INTELLIGENCE OFFICER**
> You are too valuable Rene and you need to leave pretty quickly or surely you will be captured and shot. No question about that.

> **RENE LEFEBRVE SR**
> Easier said than done. I have 6 children and a wife than need me.

> **BRITISH INTELLIGENCE OFFICER**
> Wouldn't you rather you be alive to see them grow up?

> **RENE LEFEBRVE SR**
> But I knew eventually this time would come. Thank you for the advanced warning.

> **BRITISH INTELLIGENCE OFFICER**
> Rene we will do all we can for your family but the way the war is going this town will be under German occupation very soon. If you want to take your family with you we will accommodate your wishes.

> **RENE LEFEBRVE SR**
> Thanks but no. This war is too unpredictable and my family needs to be among their own rather than running from town to town with me.
> (MORE)

(CONTINUED)

MARCEL: The Right Hand of God
CONTINUED:

> RENE LEFEBRVE SR (CONT'D)
> Plus I will be of better service
> working directly for the war
> effort.

FADE OUT.

FADE IN:

RENE SR PLANS HIS DEPARTURE

INT. - NIGHT - LEFEBVRE FAMILY HOME

As the Lefebvre family sits to have their Dinner, Gabrielle Lefebvre gestures to Rene Sr to lead prayers. The Children are all properly dressed for dinner and the two maids assist in bringing the meals from the kitchen to the table. The children are joking and laughing during the meal as Rene Sr fights back his facial expression of concern knowing he will need to leave shortly. As the dinner comes to a close Rene Sr. Walks into his study and signals for Gabrielle to follow him. Gabrielle asks the servants to help get the Children washed and ready for bed.

> RENE LEFEBRVE SR
> Gabrielle the time has come where I
> will need to leave and join the war
> effort directly.

Gabrielle gets a disgusted look on her face but looks up at Rene Sr with a look of understanding yet still questioning the decision.

> GABRIELLE LEFEBRVE
> What will we do without you to run
> the factory and why do you need to
> leave now.

Rene Sr takes a big breath as he try's to comfort Gabrielle.

> RENE LEFEBRVE SR
> I have no choice but to leave as
> soon as possible. I had a visitor
> today that informed me I have been
> detected. The Germans know of me.
> But don't worry, I will meet with
> the staff tomorrow and Franz
> Naumann will be able to maintain
> the factory until I return.

(CONTINUED)

MARCEL: The Right Hand of God
CONTINUED:

>   GABRIELLE LEFEBRVE
>   How will we keep in touch, what
>   should I do if I need to contact
>   you?
>
>   RENE LEFEBRVE SR
>   I will have an intelligence officer
>   relay messages between us.

The servants start to bring the Children into the living room and they gather around the statue of the Blessed Mother as Marcel rushes over to start lighting the candles. Rene Sr. and Gabrielle start to move towards the living room.

>   RENE LEFEBRVE SR (CONT'D)
>   Marcel tonight you will lead the
>   Rosary.
>
>   MARCEL LEFEBVRE
>   I believe in God the Father
>   almighty, creator of heaven and
>   earth.

>   CUT TO:

INT. - DAY - RENE SR FACTORY OFFICE

Rene Sr. opens his door and calls out to his Foreman for a meeting. He is barely heard over the Loom Machines but Franz Neumann turns and nods in acknowledgement. Concern comes over his face as he trot's up the stairs leading to Rene Sr office. Other workers take notice and look up at Franz heads towards Rene's office. Gabrielle Lefebvre wipes off her hands and walks over towards the brake room. Franz enters Rene's office and Rene Sr. looks preoccupied with the details of matters he needs to finish before he leaves.

>   RENE LEFEBRVE SR
>   Hello Franz, I need to speak to you
>   about a transition plan.
>
>   FRANZ NEUMANN
>   Mr. Lefebvre what transition? Are
>   we closing the factory?
>
>   RENE LEFEBVE SR
>   No (laughing). Franz I mean my
>   transition. I will need to leave
>   town indefinitely and you are my
>   most trusted foreman.
>   (MORE)

>   (CONTINUED)

MARCEL: The Right Hand of God
CONTINUED:

> RENE LEFEBRVE SR (CONT'D)
> I will provide all the necessary capital for you to maintain the factory. I will keep you updated on my efforts out of town on a regular basis and Gabrielle will act in my capacity for certain decisions. Please do all you can to make as many of the operational decisions yourself.

> FRANZ NEUMANN
> Mr. Lefebrve do you have any concern of a German occupation of the town? Is that why you are leaving.

> RENE LEFEBRVE SR
> I do and is one of the reasons for my departure. You must do all you can not to have any conflicts with the Germans when that time comes. We do not want to give them any reason to nationalize the factory.

> FRANZ NEUMANN
> Nationalize! It could be that bad couldn't it? I understand Mr. Lefebrve. I wish you well and will keep you in my prayers.

> RENE LEFEBRVE SR
> Franz one last thing (as Franz is walking away).

> FRANZ NEUMANN
> Yes Mr. Lefebrve?

> RENE LEFEBRVE SR
> Encourage our workers to participate in Sunday mass. It kills me when I see very few at mass on Sunday. I know your concern is first and fore most the profitability of the factory but we should also be assisting our workers in the salvation of their souls.

MARCEL: The Right Hand of God
CONTINUED:

> FRANZ NEUMANN
> Mr. Lefebrve I feel I need to tell
> you that your employees our unhappy
> on Sundays because they can not
> come and work in the factory. They
> can't wait for me to open the
> factory on Monday morning. Their
> lives are this factory. That's just
> the way it is.

Rene Sr gestures somewhat sympathetically and then grabs his coat and hat and walks out of his office. He looks back at Franz with a smile and thanks him. Rene Sr then walks down the stairs and is greeted by Gabrielle with a hug and a kiss. She has tears in her eyes and she trys to fight back the emotions.

> GABRIELLE LEFEBRVE
> Rene, my prayers are with you.
> Please do all you can to stay safe
> and come back to us.

Rene Sr. is trying to hold back his emotions and gives Gabrielle a hug and kiss goodbye.

> RENE LEFEBRVE SR
> Gabrielle I will come back. I have
> the Blessed Mother watching both me
> and my family. Stay strong.

Rene Sr. puts his hat on and heads toward the front door where a car is waiting for him. As he gets to the car he looks back at the factory as if to say goodbye for good. He then turns around slowly and gets into the car.

FADE OUT.

FADE IN:

THE WOMEN ARE LEFT BEHIND

EXT - DAY - TOURCOING NORD, FRANCE - OUTSIDE LEFEBVRE FACTORY - JANUARY 1915

The war is in full force and the town see's the mobilization of men coming in and out. There is a scene in which Franz Neumann is being recruited for the war effort with all the other men in town. The next scene shows Franz with other men getting on the trucks in their uniforms.

(CONTINUED)

MARCEL: The Right Hand of God
CONTINUED:

Gabrielle and the other women are standing watching as the remaining men leave for the war. Tears are in the eyes of most of the women. Gabrielle is standing with a stern face as if she is trying to be strong for all the other women. She puts her arm around Mrs Nuemann and walks her towards the factory. Mrs Nuemann is distraught and walks with her head down in great despair.

                                                    CUT TO:

INT - DAY - INSIDE RENE SR OFFICE

As Gabrielle and Mrs. Nuemann enter the factory, Gabrielle rushes up the stairs to the office as Mrs. Nuemann follows Gabrielle into Rene Sr office trying to keep up with Gabrielle's quick pace.

                    MRS NUEMANN - FACTORY WORKER
               Mrs. Lefebvre what do all the
               mothers do for work as their
               husbands are called into service?
               What will they live on? What will
               become of them when there are no
               men in the town left or in the
               homes?

Gabrielle hesitates before answering Mrs. Nuemann so as to be sure she doesn't create further concern. She gains her composure after being a witness to most of the men leaving for the war. She must be strong in her response.

                         GABRIELLE LEFEBRVE
               Mrs Nuemann what did you do when
               you knew Franz was called to the
               front? You decided to join the
               factory in his place didn't you? So
               why do you worry about living or
               getting by while our husbands are
               away at war?

                    MRS NUEMANN - FACTORY WORKER
               Its not me or my family that I am
               worried about. I am so grateful
               that my family has the Lefebvre
               family as employers. I am speaking
               of all those who will not have the
               ability to get a job. You can only
               hire and support so many families.

Gabrielle smiles and resumes her strong approach.

                                                    (CONTINUED)

MARCEL: The Right Hand of God
CONTINUED:

> GABRIELLE LEFEBRVE
> Mrs. Nuemann let the future happen.
> We will do what we can. I am in
> contact with the Ursuline Sisters
> and they will be able to assist if
> the matter becomes dire.

> MRS NUEMANN - FACTORY WORKER
> Not to sound so negative but the
> schools are losing their male
> teachers and even the Churches
> their Priests. Its as if all men
> from every form of life are going
> to the front. We can't continue
> without our men!

> GABRIELLE LEFEBRVE
> In that regard I will repeat what
> Rene said to me before going off to
> the front. Rely on our Blessed
> Mother and continue the devotions.
> The rest is in Gods hands. Be
> strong if not for yourself than for
> the other women and your family.
> They are watching.

Gabrielle puts her arm around Mrs. Nuemann as to provide her comfort as she walks her to the door. As Mrs. Nuemann leaves the office and the door is closed behind her, Gabrielle turns and her real feelings of concern come over her. She looks at Rene's desk realizing that she will be the one to take over for Franz. She stares at the picture of the Blessed Mother on the wall behind Rene Sr desk and as she goes into a peaceful trance looking at the picture the office door is swung open in much commotion. Marcel Lefebvre comes running into the office out of breath.

> GABRIELLE LEFEBRVE (CONT'D)
> Marcel stop playing and get back to
> your studies.

Gabrielle notices the anguish in Marcels face and takes on a look of compassion. Marcel catches his breath.

> MARCEL LEFEBVRE
> Mother you must look at the
> soldiers and prisoners - there are
> so many. Come look.

CUT TO:

MARCEL: The Right Hand of God

GABRIELLE MEETS THE GERMANS

EXT. - DAY - TOURCOING NORD, FRANCE - STREET

The fighting soldiers with their prisoners along with the dead in carts are coming into town from the front. Hussars and Lancers all on horseback start processing through the streets wearing helmets and carrying lances nine feet long. Suddenly the scene moves to the German soldiers coraling the towns people into the square for orders. A German Officer gets ready to speak and he possesses a very arrogant and militaristic stance.

> GERMAN OFFICER
> Dear Tourcoing residents we need your attention! I have sign up sheets for all residents to provide housing and meals for our soldiers. Please volunteer your homes so we will not have to take them over through other means. All men, women and children will need to register by age and talents immediately.

Gabrielle Lefebvre walks from her the factory to the town square to listen to the German Officer speak. She has great concern on her face that her labor force may be taken from the factory. She waits for a break in the German Officers announcement but abruptly cuts him off.

> GABRIELLE LEFEBRVE
> Sir!

> GERMAN OFFICER
> Captain!

> GABRIELLE LEFEBRVE
> Sorry Captain. I am Gabrielle Lefebrve and I own the textile factory (as she points) across the street.

> GERMAN OFFICER
> Yes Madam? (in a frustrated tone for being interrupted)

> GABRIELLE LEFEBRVE
> Sir do I need to be concerned with loss of my employees? Will you be using them for the war effort?

(CONTINUED)

MARCEL: The Right Hand of God
CONTINUED:

> GERMAN OFFICER
> Madam we may. Please step back and
> I will visit your plant soon enough
> to determine how your workers and
> your plant will be utilized.

Gabrielle looks as if she wants to respond but catches herself. The German officer gives her a look that it would be much smarter if she didn't say anything to challenge him. Mrs. Nuemann looks directly at Gabrielle with a gesture to be quiet and not to upset the German Officer. Gabrielle returns a frustrated but submissive response. Then gains her composure and just returns a smile to Mrs. Neumann. As Gabrielle turns to return to the factory, the German Soldiers are yelling out orders to the towns people. Gabrielle walks past a soup kitchen outside to feed the residents. She hears many residents complaining of how their is no food for their families. Up runs Marcel and Rene Jr.

> MARCEL LEFEBVRE
> Mother do you want Rene and I to
> help at the factory today?

> GABRIELLE LEFEBRVE
> No Marcel. Take your brother over
> to the Ursuline Sisters to help
> feed the people. After your done
> don't forget about your servers
> meeting at St Jean-Baptiste. Fr
> Rostand has much to do being the
> only priest in town.

> MARCEL LEFEBVRE
> Yes Mother but why are the German
> soldiers searching all the homes
> and factories in town? Will they be
> searching the Churches as well?

> GABRIELLE LEFEBRVE
> They are making sure that everyone
> is accounted for so there will be
> enough food for all. Go along and
> don't worry about the soldiers just
> make sure you learn your Latin.

FADE TO:

GABRIELLE IS WARNED

MARCEL: The Right Hand of God

INT. - DAY - LEFEBVRE FACTORY - OFFICE

AS GABRIELLE IS REVIEWING PURCHASING RECORDS WITH ONE OF HER WORKERS THE GERMAN OFFICER BARGES IN.

> GABRIELLE LEFEBRVE
> Mrs Prange can you ...

> GERMAN OFFICER
> Madam .....?

> GABRIELLE LEFEBRVE
> Lefebrve.. Gabrielle Lefebrve

> GERMAN OFFICER
> Yes Mrs Lefebrve, please excuse my interruption but I have much to do and little time to do it. I need for you to provide me a complete breakdown of all your purchases on a weekly basis. I also need to know if you have any wool for the war effort. Nobody will be allowed to have wool unreported. Do you understand?

> GABRIELLE LEFEBRVE
> Yes sir. (catching herself) I mean Captain.

> GERMAN OFFICER
> That will be all for now. Please do not make my job any harder than it needs to be.

The German Officer gives Gabrielle a stern look to make his point. Gabrielle is trying to act as if she is not upset by his statements and returns a worried smile and then abruptly turns away. As the German Officer turns quickly to leave the office mrs. Nuemann sheepishly enters the room and walks submissively around the German Officer. The German Officer doesn't even acknowledge Mrs. Nuemann.

> MRS NUEMANN - FACTORY WORKER
> Pleasant Man isn't he? Is everything alright? Are the Germans going to nationalize the factory?

(CONTINUED)

MARCEL: The Right Hand of God
CONTINUED:

> **GABRIELLE LEFEBRVE**
> No. But we need to remove as much wool from our inventory and adjust the records accordingly. They will start reviewing our inventory very soon and regularly. They will know exactly what our needs are.

> **MRS NUEMANN - FACTORY WORKER**
> Where should we move it? Should we hide it in our homes?

Gabrielle pauses for a minute to think and then bursts out with the decision.

> **GABRIELLE LEFEBRVE**
> No! They will find it for sure in the home searches. Instead lets hide it in the factory walls. They shouldn't find it there.

CUT TO:

THE ARREST OF GABRIELLE

INT. - DAY - LEFEBVRE FACTORY - 1 YEAR LATER

> **MARCEL LEFEBVRE**
> Mother, Mother the Soldiers are coming the soldier are coming.

German soldiers start barging into the factory with the German Solider following them in a quick step. The stop at the office door until the German Officer catches up and he opens the office door.

> **GERMAN OFFICER**
> Mrs Lefebrve are you hiding any wool in your factory?

> **GABRIELLE LEFEBRVE**
> Sir I have provided you with all my records.

(CONTINUED)

MARCEL: The Right Hand of God
CONTINUED:

>   GERMAN OFFICER
>   That is not what I asked you. But
>   if you are anything like the other
>   factories you are surely hiding
>   something. Where is your basement
>   access?

Out of fear Gabrielle can not think of anyway to avoid showing him the direction and points to the basement staircase below in the factory from her office window. The German Officer signals the soldiers to go to the basement and as Gabrielle moves to follow them the German Officer holds up his hand in a stop gesture and Gabrielle stops abruptly.

>   GERMAN OFFICER (CONT'D)
>   They will not need your help. You
>   can stay right here!

Gabrielle try's to recapture her composure so as not to signal and deception.

>   GERMAN OFFICER (CONT'D)
>   Unless you want to show them where
>   you are hiding the wool (laughing
>   with a stern look).

Gabrielle says nothing and returns a scared laugh.

                                                    CUT TO:

INT. - DAY - LEFEBVRE FACTORY BASEMENT - 20 MINUTES LATER

The soldiers start making holes in the basement walls every 3 to 4 feet and Gabrielle looks over at Marcel in her office with her arm around him in complete fear of discovery. While the German Officer focuses on her facial expression with every pounding of the hammers in the basement. The sound of one of the German Soldiers rushing up the basement stairs.

>   GERMAN SOLDIER
>   (In an excited and shouting voice)
>   Sir I think you need to come down
>   here!

                                                    CUT TO:

The Soldiers are showing the German Officer what they have found.

                                                    (CONTINUED)

MARCEL: The Right Hand of God
CONTINUED:

Gabrielle see's how they have been busting holes in the walls every 4 feet in order to find the wool and she spots the one hole with wool sticking through.

> GERMAN OFFICER
> Madam Lefebvre can you explain this to me! (as he pulls the wool from the wall and sticks it into her face as if to make her eat it) Can you explain to me why you would insulate your basement walls with wool? Can you explain to me why you should treat me so disrespectfully after I have been so good to you and your workers. Is this how you repay me? I understood you to be a good Catholic Women - Is this the evil you commit against me and the German empire?

Gabrielle says nothing and merely looks to the ground in defeat. Than in an act of courage as she see's Marcel enter the basement she lifts her head high and responds.

> GABRIELLE LEFEBRVE
> Shall I tell you what the real evil is? To cringe to the things that are called evils, to surrender to them our freedom, in defiance of which we ought to face any suffering.

> GERMAN OFFICER
> Suffering and what is that to me?

> GABRIELLE LEFEBRVE
> Truth!

> GERMAN OFFICER
> Truth - what is that to me? You are the one they claim to be religious! Or is that your coward husband that you speak of?

MARCEL: The Right Hand of God
CONTINUED:

> **GABRIELLE LEFEBRVE**
> A religious person is a person who holds God and man in one thought at one time, at all times, who suffers harm done to others, whose greatest passion is compassion, whose greatest strength is love and defiance of despair. So yes I guess that is my husband that I gain my truth.

> **GERMAN OFFICER**
> Defiance? The defiance of established authority, religious and secular, social and political, as a world-wide phenomenon may well one day be accounted the outstanding event of this decade. We heard about your husband. We know his ideals of monarchy and the Church.

> **GABRIELLE LEFEBRVE**
> Nothing short of self-respect and that justice which is essential to a national character ought to involve us in war; for sure I am, if OUR country is preserved in tranquillity any longer, it may bid defiance, in a just cause, to any power. So call me and my husband what you will, it is not us you are accountable to for your actions.

> **GERMAN SOLDIER**
> Enough of your insolence, take her away!

The Soldiers rush forward to take Gabrielle to prison. Gabrielle suddenly starts thinking of her children and calls out to Marcel who starts to run along side of her in tears as the soldiers start pulling her so hard and fast that her feet start to drag on the floor.

> **GABRIELLE LEFEBRVE**
> Marcel! Go to Dorothy. Have her meet me at the prison.

> **MARCEL LEFEBVRE**
> Mother they can't take you. We need you! (in a crying voice)

(CONTINUED)

MARCEL: The Right Hand of God
CONTINUED:

>				GABRIELLE LEFEBRVE
>		Just do as I say Marcel - Get
>		Dorothy.

>						DISSOLVE TO:

INT. - NIGHT - TOURCOING NORD, FRANCE PRISON

As Dorothy (one of the housekeepers) walks into the Prison with Marcel by the Hand they take in the terrible condition of the jail. They clearly demonstrate they never were at the prison before but how much the war must have made it an even worse place than before. Many of the prisoners are from the war. Inmates are poorly clothed and coughing from illness and mistreatment. They see vermin crawling along the floors after food thrown in the corners. They approach Gabrielle's cell and she is already in her prison clothing looking very tired and anxious. Her head is bleeding from what looks like a beating.

>				DORTHY - HOUSEKEEPER
>		Madam Lefebvre are you okay? What
>		can I do to help you out of here?
>		Should I call Fr. Rostand?

>				GABRIELLE LEFEBRVE
>		NO! There is nothing he can do and
>		I do not want him involved. They
>		will make it even harder on the
>		religious. Please make sure that
>		the children are taken care of and
>		please try to keep their life as
>		normal as possible until I return.

Gabrielle gives Dorothy the look that she doesn't want any of the children brought to the prison but does not want to say anything in front of Marcel.

>				DORTHY - HOUSEKEEPER
>		Madam we have tried to put the word
>		out to Mr. Lefebrve of your
>		situation.

>				GABRIELLE LEFEBRVE
>		No please Dorothy do not get Rene
>		involved. If he tries to return
>		they will surely put him in prison
>		as well.
>			(MORE)

(CONTINUED)

MARCEL: The Right Hand of God

CONTINUED:

> GABRIELLE LEFEBRVE (CONT'D)
> Instead just ask Mrs. Nuemann to take over the factory and work with the factory women to ensure the food supplies reach the families. I will be okay.

Gabrielle is trying to hide her pain and worry while Marcel is looking so worriedly at her.

> DORTHY - HOUSEKEEPER
> Madam, I have been meaning to tell you about the food supplies before. The Americans had supposedly sent us food: Chickens had arrived completely rotten from over there, and flour.

> GABRIELLE LEFEBRVE
> Flour is good! What kind?

> DORTHY - HOUSEKEEPER
> It was probably, I don't know, buckwheat flour, or a potato or vegetable flour. We wondered where this flour had been , because the bread which the baker made from it was black, completely black, and it would not dry out. The inside was mushy and had even come apart from the crust.

> GABRIELLE LEFEBRVE
> Dorothy, these are hard times. They will have to eat it. What other choice do they have.

FADE OUT.

FADE IN:

The next scenes are the horrors of the war as seen through the eyes of Marcel. As he is looking out of his window he can see that he is very close to the front in Southern Belgium. At night he can see the horizon completely lit up by exploding shells. The scenes move from Marcels view to Rene Sr view who is looking on with great concern for his family. The following day both Rene Sr and Marcel are seeing the results of the great battles the night before as they see wounded people by the hundreds.

CUT TO:

(CONTINUED)

MARCEL: The Right Hand of God
CONTINUED:

The German Soldiers are ordering all families out of their homes onto the sidewalks so they can select who they need for work. They announce on loud speakers that all able bodied workers were needed to work in the centers for sorting bullets, pieces of copper since the Germans were running out of copper for shells. They order everyone that are sixteen years old and older to have their suitcases packed and with them as they stood on they as they stand on the side walk. Dorothy is looking dishoveled as she try's to get all the children organized.

> DORTHY - HOUSEKEEPER
> Come on Children lets hurry and stand next to each other from oldest to youngest.

> ALIEDA - HOUSEKEEPER
> Dorothy will they take us?

> DORTHY - HOUSEKEEPER
> (in a voice of almost defiance that Alieda may frighten the children)
> NO Alieda! We are too old and the Children too young, You heard them they want those 16 and older and none of the Children are 16. You, I and Alfred are of no use because we are too old. Just be quiet and line up.

> ALFRED - HOUSEKEEPER
> I hope you are right, the Germans appear to be losing and may want to just make an example of us.

Dorothy darts an angry stare at Alfred for saying such a thing in front of the children.

> RENE LEFEBRVE JR
> Dorothy could Marcel and I be chosen since we are good workers? They know what we have done in the factory?

> MARCEL LEFEBVRE
> Rene don't worry, just listen to Dorothy. Mom told us to listen and obey her.

(CONTINUED)

MARCEL: The Right Hand of God
CONTINUED:

                DORTHY - HOUSEKEEPER
    Thank you Marcel. Now Children
    stand straight

                              CUT TO:

Scenes of the German Soldiers loading people onto trucks under the direction of the German Officer takes place. Many people are crying as they are being loaded into the trucks. Mothers are screaming to be taken with their children but the soldiers push them away from the trucks aggressively. As the German officer approaches the Lefebvre family he calls out to Marcel.

                GERMAN OFFICER
    There is the little Lefebrve! The
    one who comes from the family of
    God and defiance. How is your
    mother little one?

                MARCEL LEFEBVRE
    Fine

                GERMAN OFFICER
    That's not what I hear. I hear she
    can no longer stand (as he gives
    out a chuckle).

                DORTHY - HOUSEKEEPER
    Marcel (in a hushed voice), don't
    respond.

                GERMAN OFFICER
    (He bends down to speak into
    Marcel's ear) If you ever speak to
    your Father again, tell him there
    is no week, no day, no hour when
    tyranny may not enter upon this
    country, you people should never
    lose your roughness and spirit of
    defiance. However his love of the
    Monarchy and the Church is of days
    gone by. It may serve you well to
    remember that as well. I wouldn't
    be surprised if he was one of those
    putting this nonsense of Mother
    Mary appearing in Portugal
    (laughing).

                              (CONTINUED)

MARCEL: The Right Hand of God
CONTINUED:

The scene moves to Our Lady of Fatima on May 13, 1917 giving the warning to humanity for their transgressions.

FADE OUT.

FADE IN:

WAR IS OVER

EXT. - DAY - LEFEBVRE FAMILY HOUSE - 1919

Scene forwards to 1919 and the war is over. The entire Lefebvre family and housekeepers are all gathered in the front yard with Gabrielle laying on a couch-hair due to her calcified back injury sustain in prison. The family is standing in front of their large house in the country.

>   RENE LEFEBRVE SR
> How wonderful it is to have us all here together. See how our Blessed Mother watches over our family?

>   GABRIELLE LEFEBRVE
> Dorothy can you prop me up for a picture?

>   DORTHY - HOUSEKEEPER
> Of course Madam.

>   ALFRED - HOUSEKEEPER
> Okay everyone, get together and lets take a great picture.

>   GABRIELLE LEFEBRVE
> Rene Jr this will be our last family picture before you leave for the seminary.

The scene shows the entire family taking a picture. Afterwards Rene Sr asks Rene Jr and Marcel to join him for a discussion.

>   RENE LEFEBRVE SR
> Boys many say that I am a monarchist. I was chased during the war due to my work with the British.
>   (MORE)

(CONTINUED)

MARCEL: The Right Hand of God
CONTINUED:

> RENE LEFEBRVE SR (CONT'D)
> But the truth is that I have one allegiance in my life and that is the Holy Roman Catholic Church. But our Church will always be a suffering Church.

> MARCEL LEFEBVRE
> Why is that so Father?

> RENE LEFEBRVE
> Because like its founder the Church is meant to suffer for man.

> RENE LEFEBRVE JR
> Are you warning us?

> RENE LEFEBRVE SR
> Rene, you have chosen to join the French Seminary in Rome because I asked you to. But as you learn under Fr Colin you will soon realize that nothing we experienced during the War will even get close to what is to come to the Church.

> MARCEL LEFEBVRE
> Father what does that mean? You feel the Germans will try to take over Rome?

> RENE LEFEBRVE SR
> No Marcel what is to come will come directly from the Devil and as much as we despised the Germans they as a people are no different than us. They get misguided by political groups. Satan will use the world to do his bidding and the Church will need to stand firm as it never has in the past.

DISSOLVE TO:

MARCEL ANNOUNCES HIS VOCATION

MARCEL: The Right Hand of God

EXT. - NIGHT - LEFEBVRE FAMILY HOUSE - 1923

Scene shows the entire Lefebvre family eating dinner. Marcel is anxious to tell his parents that he wants to become a priest.

> MARCEL LEFEBVRE
> Father, Mother, I need to tell you that I feel I have a vocation. I want to become a priest. (his voice slightly shaking)

The children all give out a yell of joy with laughter following.

> GABRIELLE LEFEBRVE
> Marcel are you sure being a Priest is right for you?

> MARCEL LEFEBVRE
> Yes Mother. Why do you feel I would not make a good Priest?

> GABRIELLE LEFEBRVE
> Oh No Marcel. Actually I always felt you above all had the vocation. There is something about you that the Blessed Mother has found a special purpose for.

> RENE LEFEBRVE SR
> (In a boastful tone) Marcel did you know the Lefebvre family has given almost 50 of its family members to the Church since 1738, including a cardinal, several bishops and many priests and religious.

> MARCEL LEFEBVRE
> Father unlike Rene, I want to be a Diocesan Priest, Curate, Pastor in a Village, I was thinking of going to the diocesan seminary in Lille.

> RENE LEFEBRVE
> No Marcel! The Seminary in Rome is where you will go. You will join your brother Rene.

(CONTINUED)

MARCEL: The Right Hand of God
   CONTINUED:

> MARCEL LEFEBVRE
> Father I am not like Rene. I am not as intellectual and all the studies are in Latin. To go there? Take courses at the Gregorian University, pass difficult examinations? No Father, I want to stay in the Diocese.

> RENE LEFEBRVE
> Marcel this is probably the last time I will instruct you on what to do with your life. I can not approve of you to become a Diocesan priest. They are way too liberal and progressive. You know very well that Fr. Lienart in Lille is the ultimate progressive. No. No Rome will be better.

> GABRIELLE LEFEBRVE
> Marcel you should listen to your father. I truly feel divine providence is at work. If it wasn't for the war your brother would never have run to be with your father and would never have joined the French seminary in Rome. He would have entered a missionary congregation. It was meant to be that you join your brother.

Marcel with a comical smile/frown looks at his younger siblings.

> MARCEL LEFEBVRE
> Children I guess I am off to Rome. Arrivederci Tourcoing Nord!!!

The children all burst out in laughter and motion a salute with their glasses to his glass.

FADE OUT.

FADE IN:

RENE VISIT MARCEL IN ROME

MARCEL: The Right Hand of God

EXT. - DAY - COLLÈGE FRANÇAIS IN ROME - 1923

Rene Sr travels to Rome to meet with Marcel at the seminary. They are walking on the seminary property. Fr. Henri Le Froch walks up to introduce himself to Rene Sr.

> FR HENRI LE FROCH
> Mr. Lefebvre I am Fr Le Froch.
> Please to met you and thank you for
> blessing us with two of your sons.
> I hear you have quite a large
> family, can we expect others?

> RENE LEFEBRVE SR
> Great to meet your monsieur. Well
> to become a father is not hard, to
> be a father is, however. I hope I
> have raised them right. But as my
> wife always says "it was the
> Blessed Mother who brought our sons
> to the seminary".

> FR LE FROCH
> We thank you just the same.

> RENE LEFEBRVE
> I have heard great things about you
> monsieur.

> FR HENRI LE FROCH
> I am just following guidance of our
> Popes. Their guidance is a treasure
> trove of which I am blessed to have
> at my use. I know you have little
> time with Marcel so I will leave
> you alone. We will have 5:00 p.m.
> Mass if you can attend?

> RENE LEFEBRVE
> Thank you Monsieur and I surely
> will be at mass.

Rene Sr continues on his walk with Marcel as Marcel reaches up to break a branch off the tree. Marcel is a walking with great confidence as he feels he is part of something special. Rene Sr. is trying to provide guidance in his talks but understands his son now needs to be his own man.

(CONTINUED)

MARCEL: The Right Hand of God
CONTINUED:

> RENE LEFEBRVE (CONT'D)
> Marcel how are your studies going? Are they as difficult as you expected?

> MARCEL LEFEBVRE
> I now understand what you meant by proper formation. Fr. Le Floch and the professors teach us how we should view current events, expose errors to us - liberalism, modernism, and so many others of which me and my fellow seminarians were not aware. Fr Le Floch teaches us how we must search for the truth in the papal encyclicals, particularly those of Saint Pius X, Leo XIII and all the popes who had preceded them. It is a wonderful formation.

> RENE LEFEBRVE SR
> That is what I heard of Fr Le Floch. He is one of the last educating Tradionalist in a modern world. How many students are there in the seminary?

> MARCEL LEFEBVRE
> 220

> RENE LEFEBRVE SR
> Very good! Marcel I couldn't tell you then why I didn't want you to go to a Diocesan seminary but I think you will discover when you become a Priest how important your formation truly is. You needed to experience it for yourself.

> MARCEL LEFEBVRE
> Father I believe I understand now. For me personally, it is truly a revelation. I feel that I am being awakened very slowly. This desire to conform our judgement to that of the popes. We ask "How did the popes judge the events, ideas, men, and things of their times, of their age"

(CONTINUED)

MARCEL: The Right Hand of God
CONTINUED:

> RENE LEFEBRVE SR
> Marcel that is why our Popes are truly the Vicars of Christ. They are above all responsible for guidance of the religious vocations in order for the priest to guide their flock properly. They are responsible for every soul on earth and they can't afford the luxury of error.

> MARCEL LEFEBVRE
> Fr. Le Froch clearly shows us, through the various papal encyclicals. What had been the guiding principles, always the same, exactly the same of these Popes. It is so clear .. So very clear.

> RENE LEFEBRVE SR
> Marcel, Pope Pius X became a Saint because without a doubt all who knew him knew his traditionalism was that of Christ. His constant formation and teaching of priests was to make certain this world would not be able to fool them into believing that modernism or humanism was the way of the Catholic Church.

> MARCEL LEFEBVRE
> Since Popes like Pius X had denounced and condemned them, we also have to condemn them.

> RENE LEFEBRVE SR
> Exactly! Marcel take great care in your formation for there will come a time when you will cling to it as your last refuge. Liberalism and modernism is entering the church and our Blessed Mother at Fatima warned us in 1918 of what was to come. It is coming. You can feel it.

(CONTINUED)

MARCEL: The Right Hand of God
CONTINUED:

> MARCEL LEFEBVRE
> We are being warned that the defenders of the Church, the Defenders of the truth and the Church's tradition, bring down on themselves the anger of all who think that one must compromise with the world, that one must adapt himself to the times.

> RENE LEFEBRVE SR
> So true. And the world will not condemn error, saying "Lets us proclaim truth, but let us not condemn error". This kind of teaching has two sides to it, and it is very dangerous. See Marcel, many will call themselves Catholic, yet at the same time, sides with the Churches enemies. They can not bear the truth, the unchanging and complete truth. They can not bear the fact that the Church constantly fights against error, that we are fighting against the world, Satan, and the Church's enemies, that we are always in a state of crusade. We are in a state of crusade, a state of continual combat.

> MARCEL LEFEBVRE
> Our Lord himself also proclaimed the truth. They put him to death for it. Father, I hope I can speak that type of truth always.

> RENE LEFEBRVE SR
> Truth stands on one side and Ease on the other; it has often been that way.

> MARCEL LEFEBVRE
> You know Father I want to thank you for seeing so clear for me. At the time I couldn't see past being a Diocesan Priest. But I know my true calling is to be a Spiritian priest.

(CONTINUED)

MARCEL: The Right Hand of God
CONTINUED:

                    RENE LEFEBRVE SR
The Spiritians have such a rich history in serving the poor and marginalized. They dedicated themselves to working with newly freed slaves on the islands of Haiti, Mauritius and Réunion. In East Africa, where most of the American Spiritans now serve, they began work in the 1860s by buying men and women out of slavery in Zanzibar. They opened schools and hospitals, taught people marketable skills, and gave property to those who needed it. The Spiritans pioneered modern missionary activity in Africa and ultimately sent more missionaries there than any other religious order in the Catholic Church.

                    MARCEL LEFEBVRE
Missionary work is my true calling. I hope I am up to the task and have what it takes.

                    RENE LEFEBRVE SR
To gain that which is worth having, it will be necessary to lose everything else. How is your health? How are you eating? How are you sleeping?

                    MARCEL LEFEBVRE
All is well and I sleep just fine.

                    RENE LEFEBRVE SR
A man ninety years old was asked to what he attributed his longevity. "I reckon," he said, with a twinkle in his eye, "it's because most nights I went to bed and slept when I should have sat up and worried". Marcel, don't worry, sleep well and put much in Gods hands.

Rene Sr ends their conversation with a great look of concern in his face. It is as if he knows more than he is saying and feels there will be enough time later to educate his son.

                                          DISSOLVE TO:

MARCEL: The Right Hand of God
  CONTINUED:

The next scenes are jump shots of Marcel being educated through the years as the years 1924 and 1925 are shown on the screen. The scenes also show him walking into Gregorian University in Rome being educated by the Jesuits.

MARCEL GOES INTO THE MILITARY

EXT. - DAY - COLLÈGE FRANÇAIS IN ROME - 1926

The scene opens with Marcel sitting in Fr. Le Froch's office.

>   FR HENRI LE FROCH
> Marcel, as you know, you are
> required to perform your military
> service. I want you to your best as
> you have as a seminarian.
>
>   MARCEL LEFEBVRE
> I will Father. Can I have your
> blessing?
>
>   FR HENRI LE FROCH
> Of course! I bless you in the name
> of the father, and the son and the
> holy ghost.
>
>   MARCEL LEFEBVRE
> Father you promise to be here upon
> my return?
>
>   FR. HENRI LE FROCH
> I hope to - God willing!

The service scenes should be brief. We will show his induction and move through shots of his military service without any dialogue.

                                              FADE OUT.

FADE IN:

THE LE FROCH INCIDENT

EXT. - DAY - ROME CAFE - 1927

Marcel learns of Fr. Le Froch's transfer and is met by his Father and Brother in Rome for Lunch.

                                           (CONTINUED)

MARCEL: The Right Hand of God
CONTINUED:

They are sitting in an outdoor cafe and Rene Sr. Signals the waiter to bring a bottle of wine as the conversation starts.

> **MARCEL LEFEBVRE**
> Rene, what happened to Fr. Le Froch?

Rene Sr intentionally changes the subject.

> **RENE LEFEBRVE SR**
> Marcel how was your military experience?

> **MARCEL LEFEBVRE**
> Military experience as expected Father. Rene what happened to Fr. Le Froch?

> **RENE LEFEBRVE JR**
> We were told he was transferred due to his age.

Rene Sr. Hesitantly jumps in when he realizes that Marcel will not leave the issue alone.

> **RENE LEFEBRVE SR**
> Rene you know that isn't the truth. He was transferred because they feared him.

> **MARCEL LEFEBVRE**
> Father I heard from my confreres that he was said to be part of "The Action Française" and due to Pope Pius XI condemnation last year he had no choice but to transfer him.

> **RENE LEFEBRVE SR**
> Because all the Freemasons already in the French Government and all the liberals that hovered around them, feared Father Le Floch's disciples.

> **MARCEL LEFEBVRE**
> What disciples?

(CONTINUED)

MARCEL: The Right Hand of God
CONTINUED:

> RENE LEFEBRVE SR
> You Marcel and all your classmates. The Priests formed by Fr Le Floch in the truth, for the fight against error and evil, for the fight against Satan would eventually become Bishops.

> RENE LEFEBRVE JR
> Come on Father how can that be? Do you really think the Freemasons have anything to do with the liberals in the Church?

> RENE LEFEBRVE SR
> Rene think it through. Never take them on what they show. Look for what they don't show and what they fear. Why they fear it!

> MARCEL LEFEBVRE
> What fear Father?

> RENE LEFEBRVE SR
> Through out the world, the majority of Bishops had studied in Rome; this is still true today. How do you stop traditionalism in the Church and introduce liberalism? How would you do it?

> MARCEL LEFEBVRE
> Shut down the teachers of Traditionalism!

> RENE LEFEBRVE SR
> Exactly! The Liberals did indeed have reason to fear that among those 220 seminarians, 180 would become Priests and return to France. Then a significant number would become Bishops. Bishops become Cardinals and so forth. They don't want any possibility of another Pius X of making it to the Papal Chair.

> MARCEL LEFEBVRE
> Father how do you know for sure?

(CONTINUED)

MARCEL: The Right Hand of God
CONTINUED:

> RENE LEFEBRVE SR
> Marcel did you ever wonder how I knew so well that you and your Brother should study under La Froch and Colin?

> MARCEL LEFEBVRE
> Just your marvelous gut instinct that always leads you?(laughing as he looks at his brother Rene).

> RENE LEFEBRVE SR
> Well it is true I do have a pretty good gut, but that is due to a lack of exercise. Do you remember why I had to leave our town much earlier than most men during the war?

> RENE LEFEBVRE JR
> Yes but Mother told us that was because the German Soldiers were looking for you.

> RENE LEFEBRVE SR
> That is true. But they were looking for me because they knew I was part of the British Intelligence. Still today I maintain some connections to the British Intelligence and so if I need the real story I know who to ask.

> MARCEL LEFEBVRE
> Oh really? So what was the real story?

> RENE LEFEBRVE SR
> The Liberal French Government emissaries came to the Vatican and said: *"We do not want Fr. Le Froch to head the French Seminary in Rome anymore. He is a dangerous man, he is a integrist, fascist, ultramontain"*, and so on.

> MARCEL LEFEBVRE
> Father the vatican must have asked for some type of proof. They wouldn't go off of just rumors or accusations. Would they?

(CONTINUED)

MARCEL: The Right Hand of God
    CONTINUED:

                    RENE LEFEBRVE SR
            None needed Marcel. All they needed
            to say was he is with Action
            Francaise and is a disciple of
            Maurras. Enough said!

                    RENE LEFEBRVE JR
            Father that doesn't say much about
            our Holy Father Pius XI. How could
            he be deceived so easily.

                    RENE LEFEBRVE SR
            If there is one thing you will
            learn about all men is that they
            are mere men. Even St. Peter
            betrayed Christ. We all have our
            weakness.

                    MARCEL LEFEBVRE
            Okay Father so our Holy Father knew
            better?

                    RENE LEFEBRVE SR
            Pope Pius XI is a very intelligent
            man who has great faith, and wrote
            wonderful encyclicals.
            Unfortunately, however, in the
            actual practice of government, he
            is weak, very weak and rather
            tempted to become somewhat allied
            with the world. That is the biggest
            error any religious can fall victim
            too let alone a Pope. Never try to
            ally yourself to this world because
            if you do you ally yourself to the
            devil.

                    MARCEL LEFEBVRE
            So what is next?

                    RENE LEFEBRVE SR
            Oh! It is just the beginning. The
            Pope not only deposed Father Le
            Floch, but also Cardinal Billot.
            You know Cardinal Billot?

                    MARCEL LEFEBVRE
            Yes he was an eminent and
            extraordinary professor at the
            Gregorian University. His books of
            theology are magnificent.

                                                            (CONTINUED)

MARCEL: The Right Hand of God
CONTINUED:

> **RENE LEFEBRVE SR**
> Yep! One in the same. He was deposed for the same reason as Fr Le Floch, because he was an upright man. He would not compromise with error. For him it was always the fight for the unchanging truth, the fight against error, against liberalism, against modernism, just like Pope Pius X. He was a true disciple of Pope Pius X. So Cardinal Billot, being another target of the French Government, was dismissed.

> **MARCEL LEFEBVRE**
> Father what does this say about our beloved France if we can not trust our own Government.

> **RENE LEFEBRVE**
> Marcel, I am sure you and Rene were kidded to some extent about your Father being a Monarchist.

> **RENE LEFEBRVE JR**
> We never paid much attention.

> **MARCEL LEFEBVRE**
> True.

> **RENE LEFEBRVE SR**
> Well, the reason I was called a Monarchist is that I never trusted a Government that didn't have at its head a King or Queen that was Catholic. See when you look at how all the countries ousted their Royalty they did so under the disguise that Royalty could not be trusted. That is the furthest thing from the truth. Royalty made sure that the people always followed Christ the King. These parliaments, congresses and phony libertarian forms of governments are nothing but Freemasons in waiting. They are Humanists at heart.

> **RENE LEFEBRVE JR**
> At what gain father?

(CONTINUED)

MARCEL: The Right Hand of God
CONTINUED:

> RENE LEFEBRVE SR
> For one gain and it comes directly from the words of their leader Albert Pike. He said:

"… the World will soon come to us for its Sovereigns and Pontiffs. We shall constitute the equilibrium of the Universe, and be rulers over the Masters of the World.. This attack on Church and the state is symbolized in the 30th Degree, the degree of Knight Kadosh ("consecrated"), during which the candidate ritually stabs a mock papal tiara and a mock crown on two human skulls, crying "down with imposture!"

> RENE LEFEBRVE
> I am not telling you this for any other reason that for the both of you to hold fast to your education and your principles. DO NOT BECOME OF THIS WORLD OR CONFORM TO THIS WORLD! Stand up against ERROR. ALWAYS!

BACK TO:

> FR. WALTER JAEGER
> So Fr Gabrielli is that why Archbishop Lefebrve took such a firm stance against in the 1970's?

> FR. MICHAEL GABRIELLI
> It was one of the providential moments in his life. He even referred to it as a significant practical lesson. It showed him the malice and wickedness of the enemies of the truth. But Pope Pius XII restated they same thing his father told him many years earlier. Stand up against error.

> FR. WALTER JAEGER
> Much of this is hard for me to grasp.

> FR. MICHAEL GABRIELLI
> Well, Marcel Lefebvre was always wary of how quickly the climate could change and especially when he became a Bishop.
> (MORE)

(CONTINUED)

MARCEL: The Right Hand of God
CONTINUED:

> FR. MICHAEL GABRIELLI (CONT'D)
> When he gave talks later in his life he said "The Le Froch incident taught me to be watchful whenever I met with Dioceses and heard reports about this or that. I immediately thought perhaps they are opposed to each other because some are liberals and some are conservatives, tradionalists."

> FR. WALTER JAEGER
> What year did become a priest?

> FR. MICHAEL GABRIELLI
> As with every major element of his life, the world seemed to be going in the other direction. The same thing went for his ordination. He experienced great joy when he became a Priest just as the world entered the Great Depression in 1929.

FADE TO:

INT. - ST JOHN LATERN - ROME - MAY 25 1929 - DAY

Marcel Lefebvre is being ordained by Cardinal Basilio Pompilj as a Deacon as his Father and Brother sit in attendance watching the ceremony. The scene will focus on the ordination and then cut to Marcel, Rene Jr. and Rene Sr. standing outside the Church.

EXT - ST JOHN LATERN - ROME - DAY

The people are exiting the Church as the Lefebrve's huddle together.

> RENE LEFEBRVE SR
> Here I stand with both my Son's, one a Priest and the other a Deacon. It is just a matter of time where I will have two sons that are Priests. What more could a Father wish?

> RENE LEFEBRVE JR
> For two Cardinals?

(CONTINUED)

MARCEL: The Right Hand of God
    CONTINUED:

                      RENE LEFEBRVE SR
        Rene, I would be more proud if you
        remained good holy priests leading
        souls to heaven than a Cardinal.
        Remember always that its about
        Christ the King and never us! Some
        Cardinals lose sight of that.

                      MARCEL LEFEBVRE
        Father I can see you still haven't
        lost your love for our elders in
        the Church.

Rene Sr just looks up to the sky to check the weather and
ignoring the statement from Marcel. Then looks back at him
with a stern look.

                      RENE LEFEBRVE SR
        Marcel when is your Priestly
        Ordination?

                      MARCEL LEFEBVRE
        September 21st

                      RENE LEFEBRVE SR
        What Bishop will be performing the
        ordinations and where?

                      MARCEL LEFEBVRE
        Bishop, soon to be Cardinal,
        Achille Liénart in Lille.

                      RENE LEFEBRVE SR
        Hmmm

                      MARCEL LEFEBVRE
        What? Do you know Bishop Liénart?
        Is there something I need to know
        about him (laughing as he looks at
        Rene Jr.)

                      RENE LEFEBRVE SR
        I never had the Privilege of
        meeting him personally but I do
        know of him.

                      MARCEL LEFEBVRE
        And? (with a cautious tone in his
        voice)

                                                      (CONTINUED)

MARCEL: The Right Hand of God
CONTINUED:

                    RENE LEFEBRVE SR
Do you remember poor Fr LeFloch? Well, Bishop Liénart wasn't one of his biggest supporters.

                    RENE LEFEBRVE JR
Father do you know that as fact or hearsay?

                    RENE LEFEBRVE SR
Again with this tone of doubt. I have the benefit of being part of the intelligence circles. I get to know much about many.

                    RENE LEFEBRVE JR
And what are the detriments of being part of the intelligence circles?

                    RENE LEFEBRVE SR
You get to know too much about too many. (laughing)

                    MARCEL LEFEBVRE
And so!

                    RENE LEFEBRVE SR
Bishop Liénart is a high ranking Freemason.

                    MARCEL LEFEBVRE
Father how can that be? How can he remain in the Church let along be a Bishop and soon to be Cardinal if he is a Freemason? It can't be so.

                    RENE LEFEBRVE SR
Marcel, remember always that although the Church is of Christ you will never be able to keep those out who aim to bring harm to it. Never! It's been that way since the time of Peter and Paul. Heck even Christ had a traitor among his 12. That's why our Catholic Church will always be a suffering Church. It imitates our suffering Christ.

(CONTINUED)

MARCEL: The Right Hand of God
  CONTINUED:

> MARCEL LEFEBVRE
> But does Pope Pius XI know these things and if so, why does he not do something?
>
> RENE LEFEBRVE SR
> You are in Rome! Look around, do you think our Holy Father can control all? Not possible.
>
> RENE LEFEBRVE JR
> Father you scandalize us with every word.
>
> RENE LEFEBRVE SR
> Never! I will only tell you what I know the truth to be. I never brought any of this up until I knew you both were well grounded and have gone through proper formation. Now you need to know so that you do not fall victim to what you will eventually see for yourself.

Rene Sr. Looks around for a waiter and then signals one to take his order.

> RENE LEFEBRVE SR (CONT'D)
> Boys, enough for now. Lets have something to eat and celebrate my son's Ordination.

                                                          FADE TO:

THE ORDINATION

INT. - DAY - LILLE, FRANCE, SEPTEMBER 21, 1929

The scene is of Fr Marcel Lefebrve's ordination ceremony with Msgr Achille Lienart, Bishop of Lille the entire Lefebrve family is in attendance. Rene Sr looks over at Rene Jr with a sign a complete pleasure at his second sons ordination. But as he scans the crowd in the Church he notices the S/He devil figure sitting in a pew across the isle from him wearing a Priest cassot. They look is one of complete evil and Rene Sr. Can't understand why this priest is looking at him that way. He breaks the stare and looks back at the ordination ceremony and then looks back but the S/He figure is gone.

MARCEL: The Right Hand of God

                                                BACK TO:

                    FR. WALTER JAEGER
              So he was then assigned a parish?

                    FR. MICHAEL GABRIELLI
              Not at first. He stayed in Rome to
              complete his doctorate in theology
              until July 1930.

                    FR. WALTER JAEGER
              Impressive edcuaiton and formation.
              What then?

                    FR. MICHAEL GABRIELLI
              He asked Cardinal Lienart if he
              could be released for missionary
              duties as a member of the Holy
              Ghost Fathers (Spiritans). But the
              Cardinal insisted that he consider
              this for a year while he engaged in
              parish work in the diocese of
              Lille.

                    FR. WALTER JAEGER
              What was Father Lefebrve's
              reaction?

                    FR. MICHAEL GABRIELLI
              Obedience as always.

                                                CUT TO:

3   INT. - DAY - MARAIS-DE-LOMME - AUGUST, 1930   3

The scene shows Fr. Lefebrve walking through the streets of the
factory town. The town has long streets with all houses built
according to the same brick row home pattern. Many unemployed
people walking the streets looking for work as Fr. Lefebrve is
being asked for hand outs. One factory worker approaches Fr.
Lefebrve who is trying to get out of the summer heat.

                    FACTORY WORKER - JOHN BAPTIST
              Father I would like to introduce
              myself. I belong to your parish but
              just recently.

                                                (CONTINUED)

FR MARCEL LEFEBVRE
Nice to me you. What is your name?

FACTORY WORKER - JOHN BAPTIST
My name is John Baptist Lamue

FR MARCEL LEFEBVRE
Nice to meet you John Baptist how can I help you?

FACTORY WORKER - JOHN BAPTIST
Many people in town are originally from the Boulogne area and since there is so few work there, many are moving into town. Can you meet with us and provide us much needed spiritual guidance along with introductions to the parish? It would mean quite a lot to us.

FR MARCEL LEFEBVRE
But of course. But maybe you could be of service to me as well.

FACTORY WORKER - JOHN BAPTIST
Anything Father!

FR MARCEL LEFEBVRE
Since I am new to this parish do you know about the inhabitants of the town and how many are practicing Catholics?

FACTORY WORKER - JOHN BAPTIST
Well Father, there is a small group of very fervent Catholics that are keeping the parish alive and well as I have been told.

FR MARCEL LEFEBVRE
How many would you say in total?

FACTORY WORKER - JOHN BAPTIST
I would say that their are approximately ten thousand people in town and of that I guess about two thousand are Catholic. But, those actually practicing I can't tell you. Most likely it will be mostly women and children.

(CONTINUED)

MARCEL: The Right Hand of God
CONTINUED:

> FR MARCEL LEFEBVRE
> Well John Baptist lets start with you. We will most probably need help at Mass and servicing the Parish needs.

> FACTORY WORKER - JOHN BAPTIST
> Wonderful Father! Count me and my fellow Boulognians among your most fervent parishioners.

> FR MARCEL LEFEBVRE
> Well John Baptist I am just the Curate and not the Pastor so I need to speak to him to see how he can use me best. I hope to see you at Mass.

> FACTORY WORKER - JOHN BAPTIST
> I will be there. Have a wonderful day and good luck with the Pastor

> FR MARCEL LEFEBVRE
> Thank you John Baptist.

Father Lefebvre pulls his coat around him tighter and heads towards the parish rectory to meet with his pastor. As he approach's the front steps he steps back to take in the size of the rectory and the proximity to the Church and School.

CUT TO:

LEFEBVRE THE CURATE

INT - RECTORY - MOMENTS LATER

Fr Lefebrve is waiting inside the waiting room at the rectory as the rectory maid walks in to let him know that the Pastor will seeing him shortly. Fr. Lefebrve looks around the room as if to take in the moment of his first assignment. Several moments later the Pastor walks into the waiting room.

> PASTOR - MARAIS-DE-LOMME
> Fr. Lefebrve please excuse my delay. Much to do as you know.

> FR MARCEL LEFEBVRE
> Of course Father. Well, here I am. What are you going to do with me?

(CONTINUED)

MARCEL: The Right Hand of God
CONTINUED:

> PASTOR - MARAIS-DE-LOMME
> Well, lets see. (laughing) Honest Father you are my second Curate and to be honest with you, I did not ask for a second curate. So I do not need you. I thought I had enough with one.

> FR MARCEL LEFEBVRE
> Oh Really!

Fr Lefebrve is thinking to himself how wonderful. Now he could request for the missionary work and his Cardinal would surely grant it.

> PASTOR - MARAIS-DE-LOMME
> For a parish like ours, I do not see the necessity of a second curate.

> FR MARCEL LEFEBVRE
> I will try to keep busy nevertheless, unless you would rather ask the Cardinal to reassign me.

> PASTOR - MARAIS-DE-LOMME
> (laughing) Well that may be somewhat difficult since I am a Pastor and he a Cardinal. No. You are most welcome, of course; consider yourself at home here. We will make sure you have a bedroom.

CUT TO:

> FR. WALTER JAEGER
> Father what a difference. Today we have so few Priest and at that time they had no need for extra Priests.

> FR. MICHAEL GABRIELLI
> Well Father do you know who the first Curate was?

> FR. WALTER JAEGER
> No? Who?

(CONTINUED)

MARCEL: The Right Hand of God
CONTINUED:

>   FR. MICHAEL GABRIELLI
>   A cocky young Priest who thought
>   for sure he was going to change
>   everything in the parish within a
>   year.
>
>   FR. WALTER JAEGER
>   Who?
>
>   FR. MICHAEL GABRIELLI
>   A good looking, smart, highly
>   educated Italian Priest by the name
>   of Fr. Joseph Gabrielli.(laughing)
>
>   FR. WALTER JAEGER
>   Really? Wow! So was that your uncle
>   that knew Archbishop Lefebrve as a
>   newly ordained Priest?
>
>   FR. MICHAEL GABRIELLI
>   Yes and he actually knew him before
>   while he was at Sacred Heart in
>   Tourcoing. It only took a few
>   discussions for my Uncle with him
>   to know he was the Real McCoy. The
>   pastor was being truthful though.
>   He had two of his nieces taking
>   care of the presbytery, the
>   cooking, laundry, etc. They were
>   good people. Fr Lefebvre looked to
>   my Uncle to assist in getting to
>   know the Parish and the people. It
>   seems they were constantly visiting
>   people.
>
>   FR. WALTER JAEGER
>   So the pastor actually did need
>   more than one Curate?
>
>   FR. MICHAEL GABRIELLI
>   Yes he did. They divided the parish
>   into sections. One section was
>   allotted to the Pastor, another
>   section to my Uncle and another to
>   Fr. Lefebrve. It was a special
>   time, a time when the Church was
>   still very strong and respect was
>   always there for the Priest.
>   (MORE)

(CONTINUED)

MARCEL: The Right Hand of God
CONTINUED:

>   FR. MICHAEL GABRIELLI (CONT'D)
>   But then there were those times as
>   well.

                                                    CUT TO:

EXT. - DAY - STREETS OF MARAIS-DE-LOMME

Fr. Lefebvre is walking from door to door to visit with the people of Marais-de-Lomme. As he knocks on a door the owner opens the door and before Fr. Lefebvre can get through with his introduction the door is slammed in his face with someone cursing from the other side for him to go away and not return. Fr. Lefebvre moves to the next house and is greeted very hospitably by the owner.

>   FEMALE HOME OWNER - MARAIS-DE-LOMME
> Hello Father. Please come in and have a cup of
> tea with us.

As Fr. Lefebvre enters the house he takes off his Black Zuchetto (hat). He looks around the house as he enters and notices many religious pictures and statues and he blesses himself from the holy water font by the front door.

>   FEMALE HOME OWNER - MARAIS-DE-LOMME
>   (CONT'D)
>   So how have your visits been
>   Father? Are the residents greeting
>   your warmly?

>   FR MARCEL LEFEBVRE
>   Yes they are. Many pleasant people.

>   FEMALE HOME OWNER - MARAIS-DE-LOMME
>   Can I offer you anything to eat?

>   FR MARCEL LEFEBVRE
>   Oh no thank you. I am very well fed
>   as you can probably tell.

Fr Lefebvre gestures to his stomach.

The male home owner enters the room and takes a seat next to his wife.

>   MALE HOME OWNER - MARAIS-DE-LOMME
>   Hello Father I hope your day is
>   going well. How are the warm and
>   friendly residents of Marais-De-
>   Lomme treating their new priest?

                                                (CONTINUED)

MARCEL: The Right Hand of God
CONTINUED:

                    FR MARCEL LEFEBVRE
          I was telling your wife that I am
          being treated pleasantly, except
          once and a while some of the
          residents are not too pleased with
          me showing up unannounced. Maybe I
          should pick a better time for my
          visits.

                    MALE HOME OWNER - MARAIS-DE-LOMME
          Well I can't see how you would know
          unless you meet them and tell you
          what a better time would be. Wait a
          minute our neighbor isn't one of
          those people is he?

                    FR MARCEL LEFEBVRE
          Well as a matter of fact I didn't
          even finish my greeting when he
          slammed the door in my face.

Female home owner looks to her husband with a hurt feeling on
her face expecting him to say something. The husband looks
back at her with a reassuring smile and laughs.

                    MALE HOME OWNER - MARAIS-DE-LOMME
          Don't worry about him Father he is
          a fanatical communist. I hope his
          language wasn't too unpleasant. You
          know to him you are the opium for
          the poor. That is why he refused to
          welcome you.

                    FEMALE HOME OWNER - MARAIS-DE-LOMME
          But he didn't need to slam the door
          in his face.

                    MALE HOME OWNER - MARAIS-DE-LOMME
          He isn't a bad man. I will try to
          talk to him; we will try to settle
          things so that he will eventually
          welcome you. I assure you he will
          welcome you. Its the time father.
          Many look at the hard times and
          they blame either the Church or God
          for their problems. But I truly
          feel deep down everyone just needs
          a good talking to.

                                                  (CONTINUED)

MARCEL: The Right Hand of God
CONTINUED:

> **FR MARCEL LEFEBVRE**
> Couldn't have said it better myself. Can I ask you both to bring your Children to Mass this Sunday so I can get a better understanding of whom all my parishioners are?

> **FEMALE HOME OWNER - MARAIS-DE-LOMME**
> Of course Father!

The Female Home Owner shoots a darting look at her husband so he would not object. Fr. Lefebrve notices and with a warm smile bids them a goodbye.

> **FR. WALTER JAEGER**
> Father we are so use to our Parishes already built and families all contributing today. It must have been very difficult in those days.

> **FR. MICHAEL GABRIELLI**
> Well, it was much different then. The Church was still very much considered the safe haven for the poor and hungry. A Priest was treated with great respect but in many cases the problem you have today were very much the same then.

> **FR. WALTER JAEGER**
> In what way Father?

> **FR. MICHAEL GABRIELLI**
> My Uncle and Fr. Lefebvre tried to find out what the peoples situations were, and very often, unfortunately, they were divorced or unmarried people who were living together. The children were not going to catechism or Mass. Anyway, we had to try and bring all those people into the parish.

> **FR. WALTER JAEGER**
> Was it very difficult?

(CONTINUED)

MARCEL: The Right Hand of God
CONTINUED:

> FR. MICHAEL GABRIELLI
> Yes as you could imagine. They did nevertheless have good results because deep down the people were good people, they had to be given the opportunity to know the parish and the priests a little better.

> FR. WALTER JAEGER
> Did Fr. Lefebvre help the situation?

> FR. MICHAEL GABRIELLI
> Oh yes. See that is why what they now say about the Archbishop is so false. To know him as my Uncle and I knew him was to be with him among the people. He was a true missionary from the very start. His aim was always saving souls. He knew instinctively back in Marais-De-Lomme that as long as the people could be in contact with a priest we could regularize a good number of the families and parishioners. It was always about saving souls to Fr. Lefebvre as it was when he became an Archbishop and until his death. Today its different, its all about making people feel good about themselves even if they are on a one-way track to hell.

> FR. WALTER JAEGER
> What about his missionary ideals Father?

> FR MARCEL LEFEBVRE
> In Marais-De-Lomme?

> FR. WALTER JAEGER
> Yes

> FR. MICHAEL GABRIELLI
> Well, there were also regular visits to the sick which were quite interesting. There were the confessions, there was the preaching, there were the catechism classes, the children's club, the youth group and you name it.
> (MORE)

(CONTINUED)

MARCEL: The Right Hand of God
CONTINUED:

>   FR. MICHAEL GABRIELLI (CONT'D)
>   It was all about providing a
>   missionary approach to our
>   vocation.
>
>   FR. WALTER JAEGER
>   Seems much hard work was done.
>
>   FR. MICHAEL GABRIELLI
>   Work was not lacking and these
>   contacts with such simple, working
>   people, they were uncultured, but
>   good people and it was very
>   enjoyable at times. But as with all
>   Gods plans, providence had other
>   plans for Fr. Lefebvre and my Uncle
>   admitted he lost of bit of himself
>   when Fr. Lefebrve moved on.
>
>   FR. WALTER JAEGER
>   Where did he go from there Father
>   and how soon?
>
>   FR. MICHAEL GABRIELLI
>   He spent the years 1930 to 1931
>   with us at Marais-de-Lomme. His
>   brother was a missionary in Gabon
>   and he would write him regularly.

                                                  FADE TO:

INT. - NIGHT - 1931 - MARAIS-DE-LOMME RECTORY

Fr. Lefebvre is sitting in a chair in his room reading a
letter from his brother. The scene moves to the young Fr.
Gabrielli walking into the room.

>   FR. JOSEPH GABRIELLI
>   Father would you like to join me
>   for a late supper or have you
>   already eaten?

Fr. Lefebvre is still reading the letter and just realizes
that Fr. Gabrielli has entered the room and is speaking to
him. He sits up straight to answer him.

>   FR MARCEL LEFEBVRE
>   No thank you Father I am not
>   hungry. Just reading a letter from
>   my brother Rene.

                                                  (CONTINUED)

MARCEL: The Right Hand of God
CONTINUED:

> FR. JOSEPH GABRIELLI
> How is he doing with the missionary work?

> FR MARCEL LEFEBVRE
> Well as you probably heard from me before they are overloaded with work and there are not enough missionaries.

> FR. JOSEPH GABRIELLI
> Yes he has written you about that before. Is he becoming more insistent that you join him?

> FR MARCEL LEFEBVRE
> Well I know why my Dad named him after himself. He has the same affect on me. Seems to know how to get me to do what he wants. But he is a good priest and I know he would ask if it weren't true.

> FR. JOSEPH GABRIELLI
> Have you asked the good Cardinal or at least our Pastor about being reassigned?

> FR MARCEL LEFEBVRE
> Well, our Pastor said that when I arrived that he welcomed me with pleasure but didn't really have a need for a second curate. Now that I have spent a year with you Father I can see he was right. You seem to do the work of two priest yourself.

> FR. JOSEPH GABRIELLI
> Oh boy, laying it on think now. You know I could not have done it without you. The good Pastor is a holy man but sometimes under estimates the needs of this parish. But Father if you think you could do more good in Gabon, you should ask to be transferred.

> FR MARCEL LEFEBVRE
> Father can I share a little secret with you?

(CONTINUED)

MARCEL: The Right Hand of God
CONTINUED:

> **FR. JOSEPH GABRIELLI**
> Of course!

> **FR MARCEL LEFEBVRE**
> In spite of my brothers insistence, the missions do not attract me. At first I thought that was my calling but now I see things differently and I don't know why.

> **FR. JOSEPH GABRIELLI**
> Well Father we all think we know things when we come out of seminary but its only after real experience we find ourselves.

> **FR MARCEL LEFEBVRE**
> So true. No, I was not made to be a missionary in far away places; this does not appeal to me. I prefer to be a pastor or a curate in a village, and to know all the people as we are doing right now. I truly feeling we are doing some good work.

> **FR. JOSEPH GABRIELLI**
> Fully agree father.

> **FR MARCEL LEFEBVRE**
> But father here is the conundrum. It is not about me but the will of God. The will of my superiors. If my brother needs help I feel terrible that I am thinking about myself. Have we not been trained that it is not our will but God's that should be done?

> **FR. JOSEPH GABRIELLI**
> As much as I would like to disagree with you Father, because it is great to have you here, you are correct, it is not about our will. If that were the case we would never have become Priests.

(CONTINUED)

MARCEL: The Right Hand of God
CONTINUED:

> **FR MARCEL LEFEBVRE**
> Well that's good of you to say that. Just got my appetite back, lets go eat.

DISSOLVE TO:

THE NOVITIATE

INT. - NIGHT - CARDINAL LIENART OFFICE -1931

Cardinal Lienart just finishes a letter from Fr Lefebvre requesting to join the Holy Ghost Fathers to help with the missionary work in Gabon. Cardinal Lienart's secretary enters the room.

> **CARDINAL LIENART'S SECRETARY**
> Your eminence the Superior General from the Holy Ghost Fathers is on the phone for you. Can you take the call or should I have him call you later?

> **CARDINAL LIENART**
> No I will take the call.

> **SUPERIOR GENERAL HOLY GHOST FATHER**
> Hello your eminence I hope I have not disturbed you, is this a good time for you?

> **CARDINAL LIENART**
> Always have time for the Holy Ghost (laughing).

> **SUPERIOR GENERAL HOLY GHOST FATHER**
> Very good. I have received a request from one of your priests in your Lille Diocese by the name of Fr. Marcel Lefebvre..

Cardinal Lienart cuts the Superior General off.

> **CARDINAL LIENART**
> Please excuse my interruption but no need to continue Father, I received a letter myself as you can imagine.

(CONTINUED)

MARCEL: The Right Hand of God
CONTINUED:

> SUPERIOR GENERAL HOLY GHOST FATHER
> I thought as much. Its only proper.

> CARDINAL LIENART
> Yes and I think it makes good sense for him to join his brother since I have heard so much about the needs you currently have.

> SUPERIOR GENERAL HOLY GHOST FATHER
> That is very generous of you your eminence. We truly can use the help and we are so fortunate to receive a priest like Fr Lefebvre especially with full formation.

> CARDINAL LIENART
> You are welcome. I will send my approval shortly. Have a wonderful night.

> SUPERIOR GENERAL HOLY GHOST FATHER
> You are in my prayers your eminence.

> CARDINAL LIENART
> Thank you and I need prayers more than anything else. Good night.

Cardinal Lienart hangs up the phone with a smile and calls for his secretary.

> CARDINAL LIENART
> Giovani can you come in for dictation?

The Cardinals Secretary walks in with a dictation pad and takes a seat.

> CARDINAL LIENART (CONT'D)
> This will be a letter for Fr. Marcel Lefebvre. Dear Fr. Lefebrve, in response to your request to leave the diocese to join the Holy Ghost Fathers, yes, surely. We are of course, always sorry to see one of our priests leave, but if you truly think you will be useful to the missions, we cannot refuse your request.
> (MORE)

(CONTINUED)

MARCEL: The Right Hand of God
CONTINUED:

>   CARDINAL LIENART (CONT'D)
>   Go with Christ and thank you for
>   all your work in Marais-de-Lomme.

                                                        BACK TO:

>   FR. WALTER JAEGER
>   Father what did the Superior
>   General mean by "especially the
>   formation"? Was Fr Lefebvre's
>   seminary training that much better
>   than the Holy Ghost Fathers?

>   FR. MICHAEL GABRIELLI
>   The Holy Ghost fathers were happy
>   to receive a secular priest because
>   they did not have to take care of
>   his formation. Even though Fr
>   Lefebrve was a student of the Holy
>   Ghost Fathers in the French
>   Seminary, but it was for the Lille
>   Diocese.

>   FR. WALTER JAEGER
>   So onto the missionary?

>   FR. MICHAEL GABRIELLI
>   No he first entered the novitiate.
>   He was with two priests that were
>   all former students at the French
>   Seminary.

                                                        CUT TO:

INT. - DAY - ORLY NOVITIATE HOUSE - WINTER 1931

Fr Lefebrve enters the front door of the Orly Novitiate House as he brushes the snow from the front of his coat. Shivering he asks spots the Novitiate Secretary.

>   FR MARCEL LEFEBVRE
>   Hello, I am Fr. Lefebrve. Is Fr.
>   Faure in?

>   NOVITIATE SECRETARY
>   Yes and we have all been expecting
>   you. I will let him know you have
>   arrived. Fr. Laurent and Fr. Wolff
>   would like to see you as soon as
>   you are finished with Fr. Faure.

                                                    (CONTINUED)

MARCEL: The Right Hand of God
   CONTINUED:

                    FR MARCEL LEFEBVRE
          My God, I never knew Fr. Laurent
          and Fr Wolff were here. That is
          wonderful, I have not seen them
          since the seminary.

                    NOVITIATE SECRETARY
          They feel the same. I will be right
          back.

                                                 CUT TO:

                    FR. WALTER JAEGER
          Father, there was a Bishop from
          Madagascar by the name of Wolff.
          Are they one in the same?

                    FR. MICHAEL GABRIELLI
          The very same. When they were both
          at the Orly Novitiate there were
          eighty novices for France alone.
          Now there are none. You can thank
          Vatican II for that.

                                                 BACK TO:

Fr Lefebvre is being led into Fr. Faure office and as he
enters he spots Father Desmats sitting in a chair on the
other side of the desk.

                    FR. FAURE
          Fr. Lefebvre it is great to have
          you here. I am Fr. Faure the Master
          of the Novices and I want to
          introduce you to Father Desmats the
          confessor for the priests.

                    FR. DESMATS
          Pleasure to meet you Father.

                    FR MARCEL LEFEBVRE
          Thank you Fathers for receiving me.

                    FR. FAURE
          Father as part of your novitiate we
          will be reading the works of Fr.
          Rodrigues.

                    FR MARCEL LEFEBVRE
          Fr. Rodriguez the Jesuit?

                                                 (CONTINUED)

MARCEL: The Right Hand of God
CONTINUED:

>   FR. FAURE
>   Yes
>
>   FR MARCEL LEFEBVRE
>   Very good
>
>   FR. FAURE
>   Okay Father it is wonderful to have
>   you hear and I will have Janine
>   show you your room and introduce
>   you to the others. Your timing is
>   perfect since we will be starting
>   lunch shortly.

The Novitiate Secretary enters the room and walks Fr. Lefebrve into the hall to meet Fr. Laurent and Fr. Wolff. The Priests greet each other with great joy.

>   FR. LAURENT
>   Fr. Lefebvre! That sounds so right.
>   Fr. Wolff we knew him only as
>   Marcel.
>
>   FR. WOLFF
>   I knew him as the prodigy.
>
>   FR MARCEL LEFEBVRE
>   Enough from the both of you and let
>   catch up over lunch there is much I
>   need to know.

The three walk towards the confectionery with great excitement to catchup.

                                                CUT TO:

INT. - NOVITIATE CONFECTIONERY - AFTERNOON

The three priests are sitting at a table with food sitting on food trays. Fr. Lefebrve starts the conversation and Fr. Laurent is finishing up a conversation with another Priest from another table and turns around to hear Fr. Lefebrve.

>   FR MARCEL LEFEBVRE
>   What do I need to know?
>
>   FR. WOLFF
>   Wait Marcel, tell us about the
>   Diocese of Lille.

                                                (CONTINUED)

MARCEL: The Right Hand of God
CONTINUED:

> **FR MARCEL LEFEBVRE**
> It was a wonderful experience. Do you remember Michael Gabrielli?

> **FR. WOLFF**
> Yes, great guy.

> **FR. LAURENT**
> Yes

> **FR MARCEL LEFEBVRE**
> Well he was the first curate and he did a great job of getting me organized and up to date. We did much in a very short period of time.

> **FR. LAURENT**
> So what happened? What went wrong?

> **FR MARCEL LEFEBVRE**
> Absolutely nothing and quite honestly it was very difficult decision to leave.

> **FR. WOLFF**
> Was your brother part of your decision?

> **FR MARCEL LEFEBVRE**
> Yes he was and the needs of the missionary. But tell me now what I need to know about the Novitiate.

> **FR. LAURENT**
> I am sure Fr. Faure told you about the works of Fr. Rodrigues?

> **FR MARCEL LEFEBVRE**
> Yes he did.

> **FR. LAURENT**
> You will be reading his works in great detail.

> **FR. WOLFF**
> That's all 4 volumes of "Practice of Perfection" while walking in the cold.

(CONTINUED)

MARCEL: The Right Hand of God
CONTINUED:

> **FR MARCEL LEFEBVRE**
> Very stimulating!

> **FR. LAURENT**
> You will be walking with other priests one behind the other in the courtyard outside. In the winter you will find it very stimulating but you may lose the feeling in your fingers.

> **FR. WOLFF**
> But Marcel the Novitiate will only be for a year and then you will be off experiencing the other weather extreme.

> **FR. LAURENT**
> Marcel if you can survive the cold you will do just fine.

> **FR MARCEL LEFEBVRE**
> Maybe I shouldn't have asked and just taken it all in as is came.(laughing).

The next scene's are a series of non-speaking roles showing the priest in study and walking in the courtyard in the bitter cold. A time (month) marker should appear on the screen that show the passing of 3 months, then 6 months, then 9 months and then his departure from the Novitiate. All three priests are shown walking from the front door of the Novitiate.

FADE OUT.

FADE IN:

EXT. - DAY - FRONT ENTRANCE OF NOVITIATE - SEPTEMBER 8, 1932

> **FR MARCEL LEFEBVRE**
> Fathers it has been a great pleasure to study with the both of you.

A priest walks by yelling out his goodbye's to the priests and them returning the gestures.

(CONTINUED)

MARCEL: The Right Hand of God
CONTINUED:

> FR. LAURENT
> Marcel I understand you made your profession today.

> FR. WOLFF
> How appropriate on the feast of the nativity of the Blessed Virgin.

> FR MARCEL LEFEBVRE
> Yes I did and yes it was. I also received my first assignment as well.

> FR. LAURENT
> Where is it?

> FR MARCEL LEFEBVRE
> Bishop Tardy of Gabon already came to visit with me and said "you know, you will be joining us in Gabon"

> FR. WOLFF
> Was your brother Rene behind that?

> FR MARCEL LEFEBVRE
> Well I responded to the Bishop that I had know idea and that I would have to ask the General Superior first. He responded that he understood but that I could not refuse if allowed since my brother Rene was already in Gabon.

> FR. LAURENT
> Well if the General Superior allows are you going to accept?

> FR. WOLFF
> Does he have any choice?

> FR MARCEL LEFEBVRE
> True. If the General Superior agrees, I will go. Plus Bishop Tardy said since I did my studies in Rome I would be a professor at the Seminary.

> FR. LAURENT
> Very good and away you go!

(CONTINUED)

MARCEL: The Right Hand of God
CONTINUED:

> **FR MARCEL LEFEBVRE**
> Oh! As for that.. That is something which frighten's me the most.

> **Fr. LAURENT**
> Why?

> **FR MARCEL LEFEBVRE**
> I really like pastoral work; I really like the ministry; I feel as if I am made for that. But a professor, ah.. no, no, a seminary professor, no. I told Bishop Tardy that there must be better apt Priest and just because I studied in Rome doesn't qualify me.

> **FR. LAURENT**
> What did the good Bishop say to that?

> **FR MARCEL LEFEBVRE**
> Ah! But yes, yes yes!

> **FR. LAURENT**
> Marcel you still fighting providence? (laughing)

> **FR MARCEL LEFEBVRE**
> Never. God's will be done. Otherwise I would never have come to the Novitiate.

> **FR. WOLFF**
> Marcel we must never lose touch with each other.

> **FR MARCEL LEFEBVRE**
> We never will if the good lord allows and the Blessed Mother supports.

FADE OUT.

THE MISSIONARY LIFE BEGINS

FADE IN:

MARCEL: The Right Hand of God

EXT. - DAY - GABON - OCTOBER, 1932

Fr. Marcel Lefebvre is met at the ship docks by his brother Rene Lefebvre.

> FR. RENE LEFEBVRE
> Alas my brother has joined me! How was your trip? How is mom and dad?

> FR MARCEL LEFEBVRE
> The trip was long - two week's. Mom and dad are doing well. The rest of the family is growing up so fast.

> FR RENE LEFEBRVE
> As you know Fr. Fauret is the rector at the seminary.

> FR MARCEL LEFEBVRE
> How many students do we have?

> FR. RENE LEFEBVRE
> The students are 15 years and older and there about 15 junior seminarians.

> FR MARCEL LEFEBVRE
> I expected the heat but the reality of being in it for the first time is something. Hot Hot!

> FR. RENE LEFEBVRE
> Marcel the heat is one thing but you need to get use to the work. Very hard work and a very tough climate.

> FR MARCEL LEFEBVRE
> How is your health Brother?

> FR. RENE LEFEBVRE
> My health is fine. But that is another matter I need to prepare you for.

> FR MARCEL LEFEBVRE
> What?

(CONTINUED)

MARCEL: The Right Hand of God
CONTINUED:

> FR. RENE LEFEBVRE
> Many young missionaries who were sent here have died only after two or three years. It is hard to protect yourself from all the different insects and diseases: Malaria, filariasis, amoebic dysentery, intestinal worms, tsetse fly etc..

> FR MARCEL LEFEBVRE
> Well you need to be more candid and not hold back. Anything else?

> FR. RENE LEFEBVRE
> Sorry. Just wanted to prep you beforehand.

> FR MARCEL LEFEBVRE
> Well let me begin work (apprehensive tone)

The next scenes will consist of shots of the work being performed by Marcel in the classroom and at the missionary. Showing hard work being performed as the years 1933, 1934, 1935, 1936, 1937 and 1938 appear on the screen as shots of work being performed. During this period we need to show his 2 years as professor and 4 years as rector.

FADE OUT.

FADE IN:

EXT. - DAY - 1938 - GABON SEMINARY

> FR. RENE LEFEBVRE
> Marcel I hear you a leaving for N'djole Mission.

> FR MARCEL LEFEBVRE
> Yes and I must say I am looking for a reprieve for a year. I will be a curate once again.

> FR. RENE LEFEBVRE
> Who are the missionaries assisting?

(CONTINUED)

MARCEL: The Right Hand of God
   CONTINUED:

> FR MARCEL LEFEBVRE
> The Sisters of Castres.

> FR. RENE LEFEBVRE
> The Congregation of the Immaculate Conception?

> FR MARCEL LEFEBVRE
> Yes. Do you promise not to die here until I return?

> FR. RENE LEFEBVRE
> I survived before you came and so I will survive upon your return.

> FR MARCEL LEFEBVRE
> Yes but I almost lost you once here already. Well we almost both became one of the missionaries in the cemetery.

> FR. RENE LEFEBVRE
> Enough said! be off and be careful. I will pray for you.

FADE TO:

FADE IN:

INT. - DAY - N'DJOLE MISSION - 1938

The next scenes will show Fr. Marcel Lefebrve in N'djole Mission being greeted by several of the Sisters and Fr. Ndong with school girls and boys all moving to and from classes.

> FR. NDONG
> Fr. Lefebvre you are most welcome here at N'djole. I am a curate here and it is a pleasure to have your assistance. I would like to introduce you to Sister Mary Barbara.

> SISTER MARY BARBARA
> Hello Father I hope your travels were pleasant.

> FR MARCEL LEFEBVRE
> Thank you Sister and yes my travel was very pleasant.

(CONTINUED)

MARCEL: The Right Hand of God
CONTINUED:

> FR. NDONG
> Father we have a total of 97 boys and 67 girls. The Sisters will take care of all the girls. They are all boarders. You and I will be responsible for the Boys. We will also made rounds in the back country.

> SISTER MARY BARBARA
> Now Father, can we show you to your room and provide you with a lunch.

> FR MARCEL LEFEBVRE
> That's wonderful - thank you.

The scene will show them walking towards to Mission Rectory with the Girls and Boys running back and forth. The next scene will show different shots of Fr. Lefebrve teaching in class, then to meeting with villagers and ending with saying Mass. The next scene will be Fr. NDong approaching Fr. Lefebrve as he is walking towards a classroom.

> FR. NDONG
> Father I have some very sad news for you.

> FR MARCEL LEFEBVRE
> Is it my Brother Rene?

> FR. NDONG
> No Father, your Mother passed away several days ago but we just received the news now. Please accept my condolences and is there anything I can do for you?

> FR MARCEL LEFEBVRE
> No Father thank you.

Fr. Lefebrve starts to flashback to memories of his Mother hurrying all the children around the supper table laughing as his Father begins supper prayers and his mother looks at Marcel with a big smile. She whispers the words to Marcel "You are my little Priest". Fr. Lefebrve is brought back to the present when Sister Mary Barbara walks up to ask him a question.

(CONTINUED)

MARCEL: The Right Hand of God
   CONTINUED:

                    SISTER MARY BARBARA
              Father would you mind speaking to
              the Girls on the works of St.
              Thomas Acquinas?

                    FR MARCEL LEFEBVRE
              Certainly Sister.

                                          FADE OUT.

FADE IN:

The year 1939 will appear on the screen. Father N'Dong approaches Fr. Lefebrve as he is walking towards the courtyard.

                    FR. NDONG
              Father I understand that you will
              be leaving us shortly.

                    FR MARCEL LEFEBVRE
              Yes Father I will be leaving for
              Europe in a week. With War looming
              I am not sure it is the wisest
              choice.

                    FR. NDONG
              You will be fine Father but please
              keep in touch.

                                          FADE TO:

The next scenes need to be a listing of a series of place that Fr. Lefebrve was being sent as follows:

- 1940 Freetown, English Guinea (World War II Started)

- 1941 Bordeaux (Fr. Lefebvre drafted into service)

- 1942 Darkar (discharged from service)

- 1943 Chad (redrafted into service)

Through out all the above shots should be shots of the War as well. It is important to demonstrate how Fr. Lefebvre worked very hard everywhere he was assigned and all the experiences he gained throughout.

                                          CUT TO:

MARCEL: The Right Hand of God

EXT. - DAY - GABON - 1943

The next scene picks up with Fr. Lefebrve returning to Gabon and he is reunited with his brother Rene in .

FR RENE LEFEBRVE
Dear Brother you are a sight for sore eyes!

FR MARCEL LEFEBVRE
Brother after the last 3 years 5 years I never thought I would see you again.

FR. RENE LEFEBVRE
Have you seen or heard anything about the family? How is Father?

FR MARCEL LEFEBVRE
I saw him and the family briefly 3 years ago. All were well.

FR. RENE LEFEBVRE
I am concerned because I know Father must be part of British Intelligence and the way this war is going for Hitler, God only knows what Father could have going on right now.

FR MARCEL LEFEBVRE
Rene you know our Father, he will never stop as long as there is a cause to fight for, but I do pray for him constantly for the very same reason.

FR RENE LEFEBRVE
Well you are coming back at a very precarious time.

FR MARCEL LEFEBVRE
Why? I thought the French and British troops had things under control.

FR RENE LEFEBRVE
Well with General de Gaulle's troops you never know.
(MORE)

(CONTINUED)

MARCEL: The Right Hand of God
CONTINUED:

> FR RENE LEFEBRVE (CONT'D)
> The English are assisting but its all the Communists and convicts that are pouring in at the same time. We are suffering quite a bit.

> FR MARCEL LEFEBVRE
> I understand the French are fighting each other here as well.

> FR. RENE LEFEBVRE
> Yes that's true. But what is even more concerning is the detention of Bishop Tardy.

> FR MARCEL LEFEBVRE
> De Gaulle is detaining the Bishop? For what reason?

> FR. RENE LEFEBVRE
> This is what is so embarrassing. The poor black people see us French acting in such a manner it truly scandalizes our ministry.

> FR MARCEL LEFEBVRE
> What can we do?

> FR. RENE LEFEBVRE
> Well, we will have to negotiate the Bishop's release pretty quickly. You ready to dive in or do you need a few days to get your feet under you?

> FR MARCEL LEFEBVRE
> Please brother! Like we will ever have enough time to be ready with this war changing everything on a daily basis. Let's go.

The next scene should show the two Priests boarding the ship where Bishop Tardy is being held and negotiating with General de Gaulle for the release. There will be no dialogue for this piece but instead just shots of the activities going on with a final shot of both the Priests taking the Bishop by the arm and escorting him down the ship gang-plank towards the Mission.

                                                FADE OUT.

FADE IN:

MARCEL: The Right Hand of God

INT. - NIGHT - GABON - BISHOPS QUARTERS

The Bishop is sitting behind his desk looking cleaned up from his ordeal on the ship but still somewhat disheveled in his speech. Fr. Marcel Lefebrve and Fr. Rene Lefebvre are walked in by the Bishops secretary as they take seats on the other side of the Bishop desk. Fr. Marcel Lefebrve looks at the Bishop with great concern.

                  BISHOP TARDY
Marcel why the look of gloom in your face? Something I should know?

                  FR MARCEL LEFEBVRE
No. No. your eminence just can not believe our own countrymen can be so disrespectful to the Church. To you your eminence!

                  BISHOP TARDY
Marcel if Christ's own people can have him scourged and crucified, who am I? Remember the times that we are living through Marcel.

                  FR MARCEL LEFEBVRE
I understand your eminence, I ....

                  BISHOP TARDY
No Marcel I don't think you do. Are you keeping up with what is going on around the world? This war is going to create an apostasy as never seen before. Our real war will start after this one ends.

                  FR MARCEL LEFEBVRE
I have heard and seen the atrocities in my travels. It is as if Satan himself is in command of this war.

                  BISHOP TARDY
So well said Marcel. Have you heard the story of Fr. Maximilian Kolbe?

                  FR MARCEL LEFEBVRE
The Franciscan Friar?

(CONTINUED)

MARCEL: The Right Hand of God
CONTINUED:

> BISHOP TARDY
> Yes. Did you know of his great devotion to the Blessed Mother?

> FR MARCEL LEFEBVRE
> I did your eminence, I read his works as well. He was an Apostle of Consecration to Mary.

> BISHOP TARDY
> Yes.
> Did you ever hear about the vision he had when he was a child? He said "That night, I asked the Mother of God what was to become of me. Then she came to me holding two crowns, one white, the other red. She asked me if I was willing to accept either of these crowns. The white one meant that I should persevere in purity, and the red that I should become a martyr. I said that I would accept them both."
> You know he gave his life in a concentration camp by asking them to take his life instead of another prisoner?

> FR MARCEL LEFEBVRE
> Yes.

> BISHOP TARDY
> And all I had to endure were a couple weeks on a ship. Not much to be said for that. Did you ever hear about Fr. Jozef Cebula?

> FR MARCEL LEFEBVRE
> No I have not your eminence.

> BISHOP TARDY
> He was a Polish Oblate who was killed in the Mauthausen Concentration Camp in 1941 as well. He was arrested simply because he was a priest. Much for the same reason I was detained.
> (MORE)

(CONTINUED)

MARCEL: The Right Hand of God
CONTINUED:

> BISHOP TARDY (CONT'D)
> The difference being that he was not on a boat but in a concentration camp where he had to pound rocks and carry these 60 lbs rocks (his voice breaks with emotion) and climb 144 step staircase called the "Death Stairs" while he was being beaten and insulted by his tormentors. Do you know how he died?

> FR MARCEL LEFEBVRE
> Sheer exhaustion from the abuse I would imagine your eminence.

> BISHOP TARDY
> No! He was ordered to run with a rock on his back, towards the camps barb wire fence. A guard fired with his submachine gun and declared Jozef "was shot while trying to escape".

> FR RENE LEFEBRVE
> How terrible.

> BISHOP TARDY
> They then didn't even allow him a Catholic Mass and Burial. Instead they took his body to a crematorium and burned it. That was 3 months before the death of Fr. Maximilian Kolbe. I could provide you hundreds of these types of attacks on the Priests, Sisters and Church. So as for me? Well I was treated like royalty in my captivity compared to these saints.

> FR MARCEL LEFEBVRE
> Your eminence our Lord and his Mother have other plans for you. They needed to you to remain to carry on.

> BISHOP TARDY
> I suppose so. Just keep a watchful eye Marcel because in your travels you will see much and the works of Satan are everywhere.
> (MORE)

(CONTINUED)

MARCEL: The Right Hand of God
CONTINUED:

> **BISHOP TARDY (CONT'D)**
> In the War, the Governments and even in the Church.

> **FR MARCEL LEFEBVRE**
> You are sounding like my Father your eminence.

> **BISHOP TARDY**
> Your Father is a great man Marcel and a wise man. He above all knows what is going on under the name of peace and coalition. No, you must be vigilant more than ever. But that is not the reason I called you here.

> **FR MARCEL LEFEBVRE**
> What is it your eminence? What do you need?

> **BISHOP TARDY**
> You will remain here at Gabon for a short time. I will need you to go to various missions that I feel we need more support. I will be sending you to Liberville and then to the Donguila Mission, and Lambarene'

> **FR MARCEL LEFEBVRE**
> Yes your eminence. Isn't Lambarene' where Doctor Schweitzer is most active?

> **BISHOP TARDY**
> Yes it is. He is a pretty fascinating man. Great musician, performer of Bach, a Doctor and a Protestant pastor. He has been a professor at the Protestant University of Strasbourg as well. You will find the Doctor very friendly to us Catholic's. Maybe you can see way to his conversion (laughing).

> **FR. RENE LEFEBVRE**
> Your eminence is there anything you wish to speak to me about?

(CONTINUED)

MARCEL: The Right Hand of God
CONTINUED:

>   BISHOP TARDY
> I am sorry Rene, yes I need you to
> know how much respect and
> appreciation I have for you. You
> are a living saint for enduring
> Gabon for so long. I know you have
> seen much death in all the years
> here. You have endured so much. I
> need you to remain because without
> you there is no Gabon Missionary.
> Is that okay or do you wish a
> transfer. God knows you deserve it.
>
>   FR. RENE LEFEBVRE
> Your eminence I have been here so
> long I don't know what I would do
> without Gabon. I am more than happy
> to remain. Just one favor. Please
> allow my brother to return.
>
>   BISHOP TARDY
> Rene I could think of know better
> Mission than a Lefebvre Mission. I
> will do all in my power to return
> your Brother to Gabon.

DISSOLVE TO:

EXT. - DAY - GABON MISSION - 1945

Fr. Lefebrve is in a motor boat making rounds with a few children along.

>   GABON MISSION - MALE BOY
> Father ahead there is a pirogue
> from the mission. He is coming from
> the mission!
>
>   FR MARCEL LEFEBVRE
> From the Mission? Why? What is the
> matter? What are they coming to do?
> Do they have news to give? The last
> time I received news from a Pirogue
> it was to report my fathers death
> in the concentration camp.

The pirogue pulls his boat along side Fr. Lefebvre's boat struggling to tie the rope to he boat.

(CONTINUED)

MARCEL: The Right Hand of God
CONTINUED:

> PIROGUE
> Father there is an urgent letter which came for you! Do you want me to read it?

> FR MARCEL LEFEBVRE
> Yes please!

> PIROGUE
> It is from Fr. Laurent.

> FR MARCEL LEFEBVRE
> From the Noviate?

> PIROGUE
> Yes father. He is the provincial of France now. He has asked Bishop Tardy to release you from Gabon so you can be appointed the rector of the seminary of philosophy at Mortain.

Fr. Lefebvre faces goes ashen and he takes on a very sad expression.

> PIROGUE (CONT'D)
> Is there something wrong Father?

> FR MARCEL LEFEBVRE
> No. No nothing is wrong. Thank you for rushing out to me.

> PIROGUE
> My pleasure father.

CUT TO:

INT. - NIGHT - GABON SEMINARY - FR RENE'S ROOM

Fr. Marcel Lefebvre is sitting on the edge of Fr. Rene Lefebvre bed as Fr. Rene sits at his desk. Fr. Marcel looks distraught as he talks to his brother.

> FR. RENE LEFEBVRE
> Marcel the appointment is in Mortain and not Siberia! What's wrong with you, you will be back in Europe!

(CONTINUED)

MARCEL: The Right Hand of God
CONTINUED:

> **FR MARCEL LEFEBVRE**
> Rene you and I are missionaries. This is what we know. This is what we are good at. I surely thought our Lord wanted me here.

> **FR. RENE LEFEBVRE**
> Still fighting divine providence aren't you?

> **FR MARCEL LEFEBVRE**
> No its not that. Of course I will be obedient to my superiors and accordingly our Lord. But, what do we have in Europe? Mother passed away, father had died in a German Concentration Camp and our sisters and brothers are all settled in their lives.

> **FR RENE LEFEBRVE**
> I know your heart is here in Gabon but Gabon over France? Never ...

> **FR MARCEL LEFEBVRE**
> That's right! I would remain in Gabon for good without ever returning to France. I am a missionary! I left my position as a curate to be here with you. I thought for sure I was cut out to be pastoral in a small European town, but this is truly where God needs me.

> **FR. RENE LEFEBVRE**
> (laughing) Marcel, Marcel, Marcel of course I don't want you to leave but even I know that if God wants you back in Europe there must be a good reason for it. Make this transfer with joy and be open to it or otherwise you will just waste good experiences by sulking over it.

> **FR MARCEL LEFEBVRE**
> Your right. There was also a reason you were older than I and why you were named Rene after dad. You have his same outlook on life.

(CONTINUED)

MARCEL: The Right Hand of God
CONTINUED:

                FR RENE LEFEBRVE
        Speaking of Father, I finally found
        out why he was incarcerated and how
        he died in the Concentration camps.

                Fr MARCEL LEFEBVRE
        How?

At his point start showing scenes of the Sonnenburg concentration camp and focus on all the Christian killed. There is a shot of the camp with bodies piled up on Rene Lefebvre's Winikpedia site. I want to emphasize the number of Christian that were killed by the Germans since this point is very rarely shown and usually all focus is Jewish atrocities in the concentration camps.

                FR. RENE LEFEBVRE
        He was taken to the Sonnenburg Camp
        in the Province of Brandenburg.

                FR MARCEL LEFEBVRE
        Where is that?

                FR. RENE LEFEBVRE
        Western part of Poland. He was
        imprisoned by the German Gestapo
        because of his work for the French
        Resistance and British
        Intelligence.

                FR MARCEL LEFEBVRE
        I knew it had to be part of the
        British Intelligence. Just like the
        first war.

                FR. RENE LEFEBVRE
        When the Nazi's occupied France, he
        resumed this work, helping soldiers
        and escaped prisoners return to
        unoccupied parts of France and
        London. He was arrested and
        sentenced to death in Berlin on May
        28 1942, for "complicity with the
        enemy and recruitment of young
        people to bear arms against the
        Greater German Reich".

                Fr MARCEL LEFEBVRE
        But I received the news in 1944,
        last year.

                                          (CONTINUED)

MARCEL: The Right Hand of God
CONTINUED:

> **FR RENE LEFEBRVE**
> He did die in 1944 after his sentence of death in 1942, He was later sent to KZ Sonnenburg, a former prison converted into a concentration camp, mainly holding Communist and Social Democrat activists. He died on March 4, 1944 in Sonnenburg after one year of terrible sufferings and privations; and when we requested his body they stated his body has never been recovered.

> **FR MARCEL LEFEBVRE**
> Rene it is so hard for me to believe that Father is gone and to go that way. He was such a good man.

> **FR. RENE LEFEBVRE**
> But Marcel it was not just our Father. I hear that during the liberation of camps they have determined close to 30 Millions Christians and 10 Million Jews were murdered or died. The Polish and Hungarians lost the most.

> **FR MARCEL LEFEBVRE**
> Do you remember how Father use to tell us about the dialogue that Pope Leo overheard in his chapel between the Devil and Christ?

> **FR RENE LEFEBRVE**
> Yes he would always remind us when we groaned about saying the prayer to St. Michael every night before bed.

> **FR MARCEL LEFEBVRE**
> I truly feel that Satan himself is walking the earth today. Things that happened during the war and in those Camps are not of human origin. Only the Devil can fill men with such hate and scorn for other men.

(CONTINUED)

MARCEL: The Right Hand of God
CONTINUED:

> FR RENE LEFEBRVE
> Well Marcel maybe that is part of the reason you are going home. There is a plan for you there.

> FR MARCEL LEFEBVRE
> Okay Father (laughing) I will take my transfer with the zeal it deserves.

> FR RENE LEFEBRVE
> Well we are not going to solve all the worlds problems tonight. But we can say a Rosary for Mom and Dads intentions.

> FR MARCEL LEFEBVRE
> Sure thing.

Both Priests drop to their knees and start the Rosary as they look to a statue of the Blessed Mother and a picture of the Sacred Heart of Jesus behind the statue.

FADE OUT.

FADE IN:

INT. - DAY - SEMINARY AT MORTAIN - JUNE 1947

Fr. Lefebvre is sitting behind his desk in the seminary when the vice-rector knocks and walks into the room.

> MORTAIN VICE RECTOR
> Fr. Lefebvre the superior general is on the phone and wants to speak with you.

> FR MARCEL LEFEBVRE
> Thank you Father.

Fr. Lefebrve leaves the room and enters a separate small room with a phone on the desk.

> FR MARCEL LEFEBVRE (CONT'D)
> Yes your excellency how can I help you?

> BISHOP LE HUNSEC
> Father are you sitting down?

(CONTINUED)

MARCEL: The Right Hand of God
CONTINUED:

>   FR MARCEL LEFEBVRE
> Yes (shaky voice), did something
> happen to Rene?
>
>   BISHOP LE HUNSEC
> No (laughing) this is good news.
> You have been appointed Vicar
> apostolic of Dakar!
>
>   FR MARCEL LEFEBVRE
> Your excellency isn't a Vicar
> Apostolic mean Bishop of Dakar,
> practically speaking of course?
>
>   BISHOP LE HUNSEC
> Yes it does! So I need to get use
> to calling you your excellency. Are
> you excited about the promotion?

Fr. Lefebvre has flashback to his Father discussing the
pressures that come with the Bishops and Cardinals.

>   BISHOP LE HUNSEC (CONT'D)
> Father are you still there?
>
>   FR MARCEL LEFEBVRE
> Yes your excellency, I am sorry, I
> was just wondering why me? I never
> felt I was Vicar Apostolic or
> Bishop material.
>
>   BISHOP LE HUNSEC
> Father I understand your concern.
> It is a common feeling for every
> Priest prior to accepting a
> promotion like this. But is there
> anything else concerning you about
> the promotion?
>
>   FR MARCEL LEFEBVRE
> Well... your Excellency... as you
> know I came from Gabon and spent 13
> years there. I know all the
> priests, the missions and language.
> I would immediately have good
> contacts with the Fathers and the
> whole Catholic community of Gabon.
> But Dakar?....

(CONTINUED)

MARCEL: The Right Hand of God
CONTINUED:

> **BISHOP LE HUNSEC**
> That too I understand Father. Going to Dakar you will be out of your element. You would see mostly only Moslems; not many Fathers and not many Catholic Centers. But Father you know Divine Providence plays so strongly in everything we do as religious. It's God's will and not our's.

> **FR MARCEL LEFEBVRE**
> Yes but of course your excellence. Please excuse my unappreciative tone. I will do as instructed as the will of God.

> **BISHOP LE HUNSEC**
> Very good! Do you have any questions for me?

> **FR MARCEL LEFEBVRE**
> Yes your excellency. Do you know the actual demographics in Dakar?

> **BISHOP LE HUNSEC**
> Yes. There are 3.5 Million inhabitants in Dakar and 3 Million are Moslems, 50 thousand Catholics and the remainder are animists.

> **FR MARCEL LEFEBVRE**
> Okay. What are the next steps your excellency?

> **BISHOP LE HUNSEC**
> You will go to Paris to meet with your Superior General to decide which Bishop will consecrate you as Bishop. Other than that the only thing I can tell you is how to be prepared to be a Vicar Apostolic / Bishop.

> **FR MARCEL LEFEBVRE**
> In what way your excellency?

(CONTINUED)

MARCEL: The Right Hand of God
CONTINUED:

> BISHOP LE HUNSEC
> (soft voice with compassion in tone) Marcel you are so use to being around the people on a daily basis and often hourly basis. But Bishops are removed from direct contact. It is as if you will be put on a pedestal and very few contacts. However, with that comes great responsibility. The spiritual responsibility of an entire Diocese is not a small thing. Do you understand?

> FR MARCEL LEFEBVRE
> Yes I do your excellency. Thank you so much for contacting me personally and I hope I can fulfill the responsibilities required.

> BISHOP LE HUNSEC
> Father you will do great! God Bless and I will pray for you.

> FR MARCEL LEFEBVRE
> Thank You your excellency.

FADE OUT.

FADE IN

LEFEBVRE THE BISHOP

INT. - DAY - OUR LADY OF TOURCOING - SEPTEMBER 17, 1947

The scene opens with a scene of the inside of the Church with Cardinal Lienart performing the consecration. This needs to be done very well because we will tie this into the 1988 consecrations in Econ. The next scene will have Bishop Lefebvre giving his speech with shots of Cardinal Lienart looking on from behind and Bishop Lefebvre's family in the congregation.

> BISHOP MARCEL LEFEBVRE
> I have been so very fortune to be blessed by Divine Providence my entire life at times when I was certain nothing good could come from the events at the time.
> (MORE)

(CONTINUED)

MARCEL: The Right Hand of God
CONTINUED:

>BISHOP MARCEL LEFEBVRE (CONT'D)
>If it was not for the insight of my Father on the changes going on in the Church, I surely would have become a Diocesan priest. This I thought was my true calling. But my Father insisted that I study under Father Le Froch. Without the blessed sound principles of Fr. Le Froch I would never have been properly attached to the faith nor understood the drama that was going on in the Church, the errors contrary to the truth and against Our Lord. Since Fr. Le Froch is no longer with us, I will prayer for his soul and do all in my power to respect his teaching by imitating him in this life.

Cardinal Lienart is seen listening with a look of destain and the scene cuts out.

FADE TO:

>FR. WALTER JAEGER
>Father wasn't Fr. Le Froch removed from the seminary due to his conservative teaching style by the more Liberal Bishops and Cardinals?

>FR. MICHAEL GABRIELLI
>He was.

>FR. WALTER JAEGER
>How did Cardinal Lienart feel about Bishop Lefebvre's comments about Fr. Le Froch?

>FR. MICHAEL GABRIELLI
>It was said that Cardinal Lienart was so displeased by Bishop Lefebvre adoration of Fr. Le Froch that he called the nuncio of Paris to inform him of the speech.

>FR. WALTER JAEGER
>The nuncio of Paris in 1947 was the newly appointed Bishop Roncalli.

>FR. MICHAEL GABRIELLI
>And Bishop Roncalli became?

(CONTINUED)

MARCEL: The Right Hand of God
CONTINUED:

>   FR. WALTER JAEGER
>   Pope John XXIII!
>
>   FR. MICHAEL GABRIELLI
>   And who ushered in the Liberal
>   Vatican II when Pope Pius XII
>   refused to?
>
>   FR. WALTER JAEGER
>   Pope John XXIII!
>
>   FR. MICHAEL GABRIELLI
>   Yep! Now your learning.
>
>   FR. WALTER JAEGER
>   Not really, just asking and
>   answering questions so far.

                                        FADE OUT.

FADE IN:

LEFEBVRE THE ARCHBISHOP

EXT. - DAY - EXTIOR VIEW DAKAR CATHEDRAL - NOVEMBER 16, 1947

The scene will be a long shot of the Cathedral with the
Camera coming from a high sky shot of the south Portal and
slowly advancing with the sound of Gregorian music as the
scene gets closer to the door.

INT. - DAY - DAKAR CATHEDRAL

The scene shows Bishop Lefebrve taking possession of the
episcopal see of Dakar with a packed cathedral. The scene
will show the procession and then cut to Bishop Lefebrve at a
welcoming ceremony by the authorities and the priests. The
next scene is a conversation with a priest speaking with
Bishop Lefebrve.

>   FR. SCARLOTA
>   Your Excellency can I ask you of
>   your plans?

A person walks cut and cuts off Fr. Scarlota

(CONTINUED)

MARCEL: The Right Hand of God
CONTINUED:

> **DAKAR PARISH MEMBER**
> Your excellency, we hope that you are going to do something to give us a school for boys. We have everything we need for girls, but not what need for the boys.

> **FR. SCARLOTA**
> Please Mrs Haddad, give your Excellency time to settle in!

> **DAKAR PARISH MEMBER**
> Sorry your excellency, we truly need one.

As Fr. Scarlota politely moves her along so he can speak with Bishop Lefebrve.

> **BISHOP MARCEL LEFEBVRE**
> The boys school? Is that a need at this time?

> **FR. SCARLOTA**
> Yes there is a need for a Boys school. The girls schools are functioning very well, they are run as you know by the Sisters of St. Joseph and Sisters of Castres. They are running four magnificent schools for girls, but there is nothing for boys.

> **BISHOP MARCEL LEFEBVRE**
> None?

> **FR. SCARLOTA**
> Not a one!

> **BISHOP MARCEL LEFEBVRE**
> Well we have to do something about that. I shall first do my research.

INT. - HOLY GHOST MOTHER HOUSE - SEPTEMBER 1948

The scene opens with a priest approaching Bishop Lefebvre in the hall.

> **FR. LIEBRECH**
> Your Excellency, the Superior General is looking for you.
> (MORE)

(CONTINUED)

MARCEL: The Right Hand of God
CONTINUED:

> FR. LIEBRECH (CONT'D)
> I'm sorry your Excellency are you hungry - do want something to eat.

> BISHOP MARCEL LEFEBVRE
> No thank you Father. I will see what the Superior General wants first.

Bishop Lefebrve walks down the hall to the Superior General's office and takes a deep breath before entering because he knows there must be something of importance.

> SUPERIOR GENERAL HOLY GHOST FATHER
> Come in Excellency, come in. I have great news for you.

> BISHOP MARCEL LEFEBVRE
> What is it? What do they want of me now?

> SUPERIOR GENERAL HOLY GHOST FATHER
> Come, lets go into the parlor.

They walk into the next room of the General Superiors parlor and the Superior General starts talking as they move to the next room.

> SUPERIOR GENERAL HOLY GHOST FATHER (CONT'D)
> First, you can not say no! You have been appointed apostolic delegate by the Pope.

> BISHOP MARCEL LEFEBVRE
> What does that mean? I am the Vicar Apostolic of Dakar, the bishop of the Diocese of Dakar. Apostolic delegate? What does that mean?

> SUPERIOR GENERAL HOLY GHOST FATHER
> You will be responsible, under the Pope, for all the French-speaking Diocese of Africa. You will have to establish contacts. And it is, moreover, very simple; the Pope is expecting you in October. You must go to Rome. You will be received by the Pope; then you will go to the offices in Rome. They will tell you what you have to do.

(CONTINUED)

MARCEL: The Right Hand of God
CONTINUED:

> **BISHOP MARCEL LEFEBVRE**
> Oh My! Can they not leave me to complete my job in Dakar? I have schools to build and responsibilities to undertake. I have only been there for a year. Now I will travel all over Africa?

> **SUPERIOR GENERAL HOLY GHOST FATHER**
> You are not going to refuse! It is an honor for the congregation; we have never had an apostolic delegate!

> **BISHOP MARCEL LEFEBVRE**
> An honor for the Holy Ghost Fathers, yes, but The White Fathers, the Jesuit Fathers, the African Mission Fathers of Lyon. They will be jealous if the apostolic delegate coming to visit them was is a Holy Ghost Father!

> **SUPERIOR GENERAL HOLY GHOST FATHER**
> Yes and so! What is wrong with our order. Why not us! You can not refuse! You must not refuse!

> **BISHOP MARCEL LEFEBVRE**
> Fine! I am quite willing to accept but would you rather I not voice my concerns with my Superior General?

> **SUPERIOR GENERAL HOLY GHOST FATHER**
> Of course not! But when the Pope asks you have only one answer and that is YES!

> **BISHOP MARCEL LEFEBVRE**
> Yes of course.

CUT TO:

LEFEBVRE AND PIUS XII

MARCEL: The Right Hand of God

INT. - DAY - VATICAN - POPES OFFICE CHAMBERS

The scene opens with the Pope's secretary opening the door to the waiting room in which Bishop Lefebrve sits slightly wringing his hands in anticipation.

> FATHER PERRAUD
> Your Excellency, our Holy Father is ready to meet with you.

Bishop Lefebrve stands slowly and follows Fr. Perraud into the Popes chambers. As he enters Pope Pius XII rises and comes around his desk to greet Bishop Lefebrve warmly. The Bishop reaches for the Pope's Papal ring and knee's on his right knee as he kisses the Pope's Ring. The Pope lifts him gently.

> POPE PIUS XII
> Your Excellency it is great to finally meet you! Your efforts in Rome are legendary.

> BISHOP MARCEL LEFEBVRE
> You flatter me your Holy Father. Are you sure you are not speaking of my brother Rene?

> POPE PIUS XII
> Oh No! Although your Brother is a wonderful missionary.

Pope walks around his desk and takes a seat as Bishop Lefebvre sits in the chair in front of the Pope.

> BISHOP MARCEL LEFEBVRE
> Thank you your Holy Father for meeting with me.

> POPE PIUS XII
> It is I who should thank you for traveling so quickly to Rome in light of your busy schedule as Vicar Apostolic. But are you ready for your next promotion? Are you prepared to accept my request to be apostolic delegate?

> BISHOP MARCEL LEFEBVRE
> Yes your Holy Father. But I have one question.

(CONTINUED)

MARCEL: The Right Hand of God
CONTINUED:

> **POPE PIUS XII**
> Just one? (laughing).

> **BISHOP MARCEL LEFEBVRE**
> Yes. Why did you select me? I am a humble missionary who barely is up for the my Vicar Apostolic.

> **POPE PIUS XII**
> That is a good question. But would you believe that is exactly the same question I had with every appointment given to me. Especially when the College of Cardinals elected me Pope. I think we feel we are just doing what we do and nobody really takes notice since so many religious are doing so much.

> **BISHOP MARCEL LEFEBVRE**
> Exactly Your Holy Father!

> **POPE PIUS XII**
> Since the war ended I have been very busy trying to help as much as I can with rebuilding Europe. At the same time I look at our Church and I see something that concerns me. Do you know what my concern is?

> **BISHOP MARCEL LEFEBVRE**
> No I don't your Holy Father.

> **POPE PIUS XII**
> The liberalism that is flourishing in Europe, the world and the Church! I need to have those religious whom were trained in the traditions of the Church. Other than all the missionary work you have accomplished and all the advancements you provided for the Holy Ghost Fathers, your training under Fr. Le Froch is precisely what is required for your next assignment.

> **BISHOP MARCEL LEFEBVRE**
> Fr. Le Froch your Holy Father?

(CONTINUED)

MARCEL: The Right Hand of God
CONTINUED:

> POPE PIUS XII
> Yes. Father Le Froch was a great priest and none better in the formation of traditional priests. God rest his soul.

> BISHOP MARCEL LEFEBVRE
> Excuse me Holy Father, I was so fortune to have been educated by Fr. Le Froch but what exactly do you want of me?

> POPE PIUS XII
> I am relying on you to develop the evangelization of the whole African territory, that you not only direct but must visit. I want you to give an account of all you see and hear, give suggestions for evangelization, encourage the bishops, and also set up episcopal conferences in the different territories. Do you understand?

> BISHOP MARCEL LEFEBVRE
> Yes your Holy Father

> POPE PIUS XII
> All this will be told to you by the Cardinal Prefect of the Propaganda whom, of course, you must go and see; he will give you very precise instructions regarding everything.

> BISHOP MARCEL LEFEBVRE
> I understand your Holy Father

> POPE PIUS XII
> In any case, I hope the collaboration would be very efficacious, very good, very fruitful, and I am ready to help and receive you any time you need to see me. Simply contact Monsignor Tardi and I will make sure I am available.

> BISHOP MARCEL LEFEBVRE
> Very good your Holy Father

(CONTINUED)

MARCEL: The Right Hand of God
CONTINUED:

> POPE PIUS XII
> Now that we have the business you came to Rome to discuss, can I talk to you about the condition of our Church? Do you have time to spare?

> BISHOP MARCEL LEFEBVRE
> Of course your Holy Father! My pleasure.

> POPE PIUS XII
> Do you know why I took the name Pius? Other than most Italian Popes seemed to love the name Pius (laughing).

> BISHOP MARCEL LEFEBVRE
> I always assumed out of respect for Pope Pius XI?

> POPE PIUS XII
> Mostly because my whole life I saw Pope's Pius IX, X and XI as giants in Traditionalism of the Church. They were constantly bringing the Church back to its foundation and traditions. But Pope Pius X was the greatest of all!

> BISHOP MARCEL LEFEBVRE
> That is what my Father felt. He said if it had not been for Pius X our seminaries, religious life and congregations would have been heading right into the hands of liberalism and modernism.

> POPE PIUS XII
> So right! So very right! By the way, my condolences for the loss of your Father. He was a great man. A man of great religious conviction and determination. A shame we lost him to the Concentration Camps.

> BISHOP MARCEL LEFEBVRE
> Thank you your Holy Father. He was my rock.

(CONTINUED)

MARCEL: The Right Hand of God
CONTINUED:

>POPE PIUS XII
>Pope Pius X had forewarned us all of what was to come. It is as if the Blessed Mother spoke to him before her visitation at Fatima. He just always knew the right path for the Church. I too want that path. But, I have major obstacles.

>BISHOP MARCEL LEFEBVRE
>Do you mind if I inquire as to what obstacles?

>POPE PIUS XII
>You of course are familiar with the story of Pope Leo over hearing a conversation with Christ and the Devil?

>BISHOP MARCEL LEFEBVRE
>Yes, of course. That is where we received the Prayer to St. Michael and why we say it after every mass.

>POPE PIUS XII
>Well, whether we believe the story was actually told by the Pope himself, I can tell you that it was truly a fore warning that Pius X took very serious. It seemed he could see the changes going on within the Church and clamped down on them with all his might. However, he knew it would take more than his efforts. It would take even stronger Popes in the future to keep the liberalism and modernism out of the Church. But I tell you now. I can see it all around me. I can see the liberalism and modernism creeping even into the Holy See more and more every year.

>BISHOP MARCEL LEFEBVRE
>Well Holy Father why can you not put a stop to it?

>POPE PIUS XII
>Did you see what they did to our beloved Fr. Le Froch?

(CONTINUED)

MARCEL: The Right Hand of God
CONTINUED:

> **BISHOP MARCEL LEFEBVRE**
> I did and never understood why Pope Pius XI allowed such shenanigans.

> **POPE PIUS XII**
> Because he was deceived. The power at play is stifling. That is why I am very cautious on whom I place where. You know I have not named a Secretary of State since Cardinal Maglione in 1944. That is over 4 years ago. I simply do not trust anyone with such responsibilities to influence my judgement as Pope.

> **BISHOP MARCEL LEFEBVRE**
> Is this the main premise of your Ex Cathedra, Papal Infallibility?

> **POPE PIUS XII**
> One of them. I fear that with all the modernistic and liberal view points the Church may some day revert to one in which certain Bishops and Cardinals will have their way with it in an attempt to bring it to her knees. This is what Pius X warned us against.

> **BISHOP MARCEL LEFEBVRE**
> So you can stop this by the measures you are taking with your appointments, can't you?

> **POPE PIUS XII**
> Your Excellency, let me ask you a question? While you have been in charge of Dakar do you have 100% certainty of what is going on when you are not directly involved? Do you think now when you have even larger numbers reporting to you, you will have direct knowledge?

> **BISHOP MARCEL LEFEBVRE**
> I truly hope to, your Holy Father. But probably not.

> **POPE PIUS XII**
> Trust me when I tell you that you won't.
> (MORE)

(CONTINUED)

MARCEL: The Right Hand of God
CONTINUED:

POPE PIUS XII (CONT'D)
You will have to delegate and trust and that is a significant leap of faith on many occasions. I appointed Cardinal Spellman as the Archbishop of New York who had absolutely no following or connections - just a good and Holy Priest because I wanted someone who could not be influenced by such modernism and liberalism. But in the end, was it a good decision? I know not. I trust that the Holy Spirit will guide my decisions and that our Blessed Mother will protect Holy Mother Church.

BISHOP MARCEL LEFEBVRE
Holy Father my Father use to say, *"how can we expect to have a Church that is not a suffering Church when Christ had those betraying him among only 12."*

POPE PIUS XII
So very true. However, at least Christ knew who his betrayers were (laughing).

BISHOP MARCEL LEFEBVRE
Holy Father what can I do to relieve some of your concerns and sufferings?

POPE PIUS XII
Marcel you already have. You are good stock and probably one of my appointments that I have absolutely no concern. However, it is not me that I am concerned for since I am much older than you and blessed if I have another 15 years on this earth. It will be you and your fellow Bishops, Cardinals and future Pope's that will truly be tested to their very core. So, above all stay close to the Blessed Mother and never concede your traditional teachings for what is to come in the form of change.

(CONTINUED)

MARCEL: The Right Hand of God
    CONTINUED:

> BISHOP MARCEL LEFEBVRE
> I promise your Holy Father. Is there anything particularly I should watch out for now?

> POPE PIUS XII
> There are a growing number of very liberal Bishops and Cardinals that are starting to ask for a new Council. The war had put an end to much of the talk but now that the war is over it is beginning again. This war has changed the world for the worse. Liberalism is being mixed with Communism and I fear that even though I will never allow another Council it may come after me. Be vigilant! Be aware and as you perform your duties, that you are about to start, be very watchful because you will be developing the future Bishops and Cardinals.

> BISHOP MARCEL LEFEBVRE
> Holy Father do I have any reason to be concerned with my Religious order, the Holy Ghost Fathers?

> POPE PIUS XII
> Let me answer your question this way. If you stand by those very principals that Pope Pius X brought forth and the education you received from Fr. Le Froch, you will stay with the tradition and you will know if they are about Christ's works or worldly works. Use Pius X as your model and the Blessed Mother for your support. Then you will be assured you are about Christ's works. By the Bishops and Cardinals fruits you shall know them. Let that be your guide.

The Pope rises to signal the end of the meeting. Bishop Lefebvre rises quickly somewhat awkwardly being surprised by the sudden end of the meeting.

(CONTINUED)

MARCEL: The Right Hand of God
CONTINUED:

> POPE PIUS XII (CONT'D)
> Thank you so much for rushing to Rome.

> BISHOP MARCEL LEFEBVRE
> My honor your Holy Father and thank you so much for your confidence in me.

As Fr. Perraud escorts Bishop Lefebvre towards the door the Pope calls out.

> POPE PIUS XII
> Your Excellency do you know why I appointed Bishop Roncalli to the Apostolic Nuncio of Paris? Your Homeland?

> BISHOP MARCEL LEFEBVRE
> No your Holy Father, why?

> POPE PIUS XII
> Much like you he was Apostolic Delegate to a primarily Muslim country (Turkey). He had to learn how to work with the odds against him. He has a wonderful capacity to make those in authority trust and like him. With a number of French Bishops being accused of collaborating with the Nazi's after the occupation of France, only Bishop Roncalli could handle such a delicate situation with a good outcome. I think of you the same with the current problems in Africa. Only you can do what is required to teach the tradition. Go with God Archbishop Lefebrve.

> ARCHBISHOP MARCEL LEFEBVRE
> Thank you again Holy Father.(Big Smile)

FADE OUT.

FADE IN:

LEFEBVRE THE APOSTOLIC DELEGATE

MARCEL: The Right Hand of God

INT. - DAY - OFFICE OF CARDINAL PREFECT OF PROPAGANDA

The scene opens with the Cardinal Prefect speaking with Bishop Lefebvre in the Cardinals office

> CARDINAL PREFECT OF PROPOGANDA
> Your Excellency you will have 46 dioceses to visit. See if the number of dioceses should be increased or decreased, if new bishops should be made. When a new Bishop dies or resigns , you will be in charge of submitting names to Rome for the appointment of other bishops. That means there will be dossiers to prepare as well. You will have to establish contact with the superiors general of the religious congregations, as the nomination of bishops also pertains to them, for they must tell you which of their subjects would be most apt for the episcopacy.

> ARCHBISHOP MARCEL LEFEBVRE
> Will I have an assistance?

> CARDINAL PREFECT OF PROPOGANDA
> Yes you will have an auxiliary.

CUT TO:

> FR. WALTER JAEGER
> Father it seems Archbishop Lefebvre never had a chance to catch his breath once he became Bishop. Did he really do all the traveling the Cardinal Prefect say with only one auxiliary?

> FR. MICHAEL GABRIELLI
> Yes and what the Cardinal Prefect did not tell him was he wouldn't get his auxiliary until he himself consecrated a Bishop two years later.

> FR. WALTER JAEGER
> Who was the auxiliary?

(CONTINUED)

MARCEL: The Right Hand of God
CONTINUED:

> FR. MICHAEL GABRIELLI
> Bishop Guibert who he consecrated in Dakar in 1950. Archbishop Lefebrve was constantly traveling: visiting diocese, calling bishops together. He traveled...

Scene shots of all the places that Fr. Gabrielli states appear on the screen as photo shots with dates to show his progress through the years.

> FR. MICHAEL GABRIELLI (CONT'D)
> 46 Dioceses in Madagascar, Reunion, Djibouti, Morocco and all of French Equatorial Africa, all of Western French Africa and Cameroon. Weeks and weeks were needed for all these visits as you can imagine.

> FR. WALTER JAEGER
> It is amazing at how much he accomplished at such a young age. How old was he? 45?

> FR. MICHAEL GABRIELLI
> Yes, in 1950 he was 45. But in addition to all that, if a bishop needed to be appointed, he would have to go and see the superior general of the congregation concerned. That meant he going to Rome since that is where the congregation generally were. It was necessary to discuss the nomination in question, and without fail, to see the Congregation of the Propaganda.

> FR. WALTER JAEGER
> Father since you are a Holy Ghost Father is this the time you would have first been introduced to Archbishop Lefebvre?

> FR. MICHAEL GABRIELLI
> Well yes and no. I was actually ordained in 1953 but I was almost immediately assigned to Duquesne University in Pittsburgh, Pennsylvania.
> (MORE)

(CONTINUED)

MARCEL: The Right Hand of God
CONTINUED:

FR. MICHAEL GABRIELLI (CONT'D)
I met Archbishop on his visits much later to the states in the 1960's and or when I was in Rome during the late 1950's and 1960's. See by the time Vatican II was officially closed Archbishop Lefebvre was ready to retire. But I am getting ahead of myself. His work during the 1950's was unbelievably productive.

FR. WALTER JAEGER
Sorry Father for side tracking you.

FR. MICHAEL GABRIELLI
No its my fault. At my age I tend to wander. Archbishop Lefebrve was also responsible for establishing the apostolic delegation, which is different from the diocese. The apostolic delegation was needed as well as the bishopric.

FR. WALTER JAEGER
So very different from the way both the religious orders and the diocesan Priests, Bishop and Cardinal operate today.

FR. MICHAEL GABRIELLI
But of course. The life of a Priest, Bishop and Cardinal prior to Vatican II was a different world.

FR. WALTER JAEGER
As for the Sisters and Brothers what was his responsibilities or was that handled by the Bishops?

FR. MICHAEL GABRIELLI
He also endeavored to satisfy the requests of the bishops who desired to have teaching Brothers or Sisters for their dioceses. He would even try to get in touch with the superiors general of the religious congregations and encourage them to send Sister to Africa, to places where they had been requested.

(CONTINUED)

MARCEL: The Right Hand of God
CONTINUED:

> **FR. WALTER JAEGER**
> They were obviously very, very busy years.

> **FR. MICHAEL GABRIELLI**
> That is what was truly amazing about Archbishop Lefebvre. He told my uncle that the Archbishop admitted that he did not expect those years to be so encouraging, even elating. He was able to see in the territory of all these diocese how much the mission had developed since 1946, between the war and the second vatican council.

> **FR. WALTER JAEGER**
> When all the negative news came out against the Archbishop in the 1980's you never heard any of these accomplishments. Why?

> **FR. MICHAEL GABRIELLI**
> Intentionally so. There was an extraordinary development of the missions in those years, actually extraordinary! Seminaries were built and the number of priests increased. Many religious congregations came and multiple foundations. Remember what Pope Pius XII told him?

> **FR. WALTER JAEGER**
> By his fruits they shall know him?

> **FR. MICHAEL GABRIELLI**
> Exactly! And later when he should have been in retirement, he established the Society of Pius X and once again replicated almost the same results. What did the others produce?

> **FR. WALTER JAEGER**
> Almost a complete destruction of the orders, church's and congregations.

(CONTINUED)

MARCEL: The Right Hand of God
CONTINUED:

> **FR. MICHAEL GABRIELLI**
> Exactly! Because Pope Pius XII had requested the Archbishop to report on a regular basis at least once a year. Therefore, Archbishop was in constant contact with many from the Roman Curia.

FADE OUT.

FADE IN:

STAY STEADFAST - STAY A TRADITIONALISTS

INT. - DAY - POPES OFFICE CHAMBERS - 1957

The scene opens with Pope Pius XII and the Archbishop having tea at a side table in the Pope's chambers.

> **POPE PIUS XII**
> Your Excellency it seems every year I am more pleased to meet you due to all your progress. When I heard you were able to get the Franciscan Missionary Sisters to work in the Hospitals along with the Sisters of St. Thomas not to mention teaching Sisters, I almost couldn't believe it. You are surpassing my grandist of all expectations. When do you eat and sleep?

> **ARCHBISHOP MARCEL LEFEBVRE**
> Your Holy Father I could not have accomplished with out your complete support for all the efforts undertaken to date. Not to mention the support I am receiving from our Blessed Mother.

> **POPE PIUS XII**
> Marcel do you remember our conversation almost 10 years ago?

> **ARCHBISHOP MARCEL LEFEBVRE**
> By the fruits?

(CONTINUED)

MARCEL: The Right Hand of God
CONTINUED:

>   POPE PIUS XII
>   Yes, so you do remember! How have
>   the Roman Curia been supporting
>   your efforts.
>
>   ARCHBISHOP MARCEL LEFEBVRE
>   For me to come to Rome I am always
>   just so grateful to be among the
>   Curia that I seem to left most
>   unpleasant matters pass me bye.
>
>   POPE PIUS XII
>   And of course that is what they
>   expect. What exactly are you
>   referring to?
>
>   ARCHBISHOP MARCEL LEFEBVRE
>   I was pleased with your election of
>   Cardinal Tardi as the Secretariat
>   of State, he is truly very
>   supportive.
>
>   POPE PIUS XII
>   But?
>
>   ARCHBISHOP MARCEL LEFEBVRE
>   But there are a certain number
>   among who treat me almost as if I
>   stole their position once I became
>   Apostolic delegate. It is as if
>   because I did not go through the
>   normal steps ......
>
>   POPE PIUS XII
>   Wait. Lets see if I can tell you
>   what they may be saying: "You did
>   not go through the Academy of Noble
>   Ecclesiatics in Rome which forms
>   future diplomats, nuncios. To
>   become archbishop of Dakar right
>   away and then, bang, apostolic
>   delegate! You are an intruder! You
>   have taken a position which could
>   have been given to us"
>
>   ARCHBISHOP MARCEL LEFEBVRE
>   Exactly Holy Father!
>
>   POPE PIUS XII
>   Would you mind telling me who in
>   the Curia treat you this way?

(CONTINUED)

MARCEL: The Right Hand of God
CONTINUED:

> **ARCHBISHOP MARCEL LEFEBVRE**
> I would rather not say your Holy Father.

> **POPE PIUS XII**
> Well it is not like I will tell anyone, so if you refuse I will have to command you (laughing) But seriously Marcel I would like to know. I need to know.

> **ARCHBISHOP MARCEL LEFEBVRE**
> Well there is Bishop Montini, Bishop Martin, your previous Secretariat of State and Monsignors of Propaganda.

> **POPE PIUS XII**
> I could have written these names down before you said them. The one who concerns me most is one who was very close to me up until 5 years ago.

> **ARCHBISHOP MARCEL LEFEBVRE**
> Your previous Secretariat of State?

> **POPE PIUS XII**
> No. It is Bishop Montini. I intentionally do not want to promote him to a Cardinal Position because his liberal views are very destructive. He acts one way but is actually leading the cause for a new council, possibly a second vatican council.

> **ARCHBISHOP MARCEL LEFEBVRE**
> Why your Holy Father?

> **POPE PIUS XII**
> Because unlike Bishops and Cardinal who are doing Christ's work through out the world, there are those like Bishop Montini who believe themselves to be the intellects of the Church who want a much more current or modern church. They take almost a protestant bent.

(CONTINUED)

MARCEL: The Right Hand of God
CONTINUED:

>   ARCHBISHOP MARCEL LEFEBVRE
> To be perfectly honest with you Holy Father I have been noticing this element in Rome for quite some years.

>   POPE PIUS XII
> I have refused this council on many occasions but I am certain after my death the Curia will be very active in their election of a Pope who will call such a council. That is why I do not want the Montini's of the Curia to become Cardinals. I fear their election through the College of Cardinals.

>   ARCHBISHOP MARCEL LEFEBVRE
> Your Holy Father I am so outside of this Curia circle due to my travels that I guess I never saw it from your view point. This is the same concern you had in 1948.

>   POPE PIUS XII
> Yes only it is much, much stronger now. In your travels have you had much occasion to speak with Cardinal Roncalli?

>   ARCHBISHOP MARCEL LEFEBVRE
> Oh yes Holy Father in the early years when he was Apostolic Nuncio of Paris. When I occasionally return to Paris in those year for the apostolic delegate, I sometimes meet with Bishop Roncalli at the nunciatiure.

>   POPE PIUS XII
> How did you get along?

>   ARCHBISHOP MARCEL LEFEBVRE
> Well each time I am there, he not only invited me, he insisted on seeing me.

>   POPE PIUS XII
> Very good. How were your discussions?

(CONTINUED)

MARCEL: The Right Hand of God
CONTINUED:

> **ARCHBISHOP MARCEL LEFEBVRE**
> Very pleasant. He was always very kind to me. He did however make a comment to me one time that I wasn't sure how to take.
>
> **POPE PIUS XII**
> What was it?
>
> **ARCHBISHOP MARCEL LEFEBVRE**
> He said: "*If you ask me, I don't think archbishops like you, who have a diocese , should also, at the same time, be apostolic delegate. To me it isn't a good idea. Bah! But that is none of my business, was it?*"
>
> **POPE PIUS XII**
> Yes, that sounds like Angelo. He was a very good Bishop for France and is doing a good job as the Cardinal in Venice but always the politician. But his support for many of those in the Curia that have liberal bents is very concerning. He supports Montini very strongly.
>
> **ARCHBISHOP MARCEL LEFEBVRE**
> Your Holy Father you have been so very good to me and I even at times have to pinch myself when I find I am once again coming to Rome to meet with you. I never thought as a simple priest I would be so blessed to work under a Pope let alone one like yourself. But now I am troubled because I sense you are in pain over what you see coming.
>
> **POPE PIUS XII**
> I am Marcel and it is so good of you to be concerned. But I once told you to be on guard. Now I tell you I do not feel I have many more years ahead of me. I need you to stay vigilant for the sake of the Church. Stay strong among those of you who know the Tradition.

(CONTINUED)

MARCEL: The Right Hand of God
CONTINUED:

                ARCHBISHOP MARCEL LEFEBVRE
Your Holy Father, I promised you in 1948 and I promise you now. I will stay vigilant.

                POPE PIUS XII
This council will come. Pope Pius XI did all he could to stop it from happening and I have worked just as hard during my pontificate. But the growth of liberalism and modernism is so powerful. The world is demanding it, the priests demanding it, the Bishops and the Cardinals are demanding it so.

                ARCHBISHOP MARCEL LEFEBVRE
But Holy Father the Church has never been of this world and only in it. The Church has always been a beacon and not a follower. How can it be?

                POPE PIUS XII
Marcel, I tell you that a time will come when what the protestant reformation accomplished in the 1600's through shear intimidation, destruction and murder will happen to the Church not through outsiders but by the very Church itself. Only this time the reformation will be done with a smile instead of a sword. There will be no force, but pure deception.

                ARCHBISHOP MARCEL LEFEBVRE
I can see that as so!

                POPE PIUS XII
Let's pray to God you are right, but things are lining up as we speak that make it so.

                                    FADE OUT.

FADE IN:

MARCEL: The Right Hand of God

DAY - NIGHT - DAKAR - OCTOBER 9, 1959

The Archbishop is meeting with several Bishops when his secretary knocks on the door but doesn't wait to be invited into the room.

> ARCHBISHOP DAKAR SECRETARY
> Your Excellency! I have urgent
> news! Our Holy Father has died.

> ARCHBISHOP MARCEL LEFEBVRE
> Who told you this? Where did you
> get the news?

> ARCHBISHOP DAKAR SECRETARY
> It came through telex your
> excellency from Rome. Will you be
> requested to leave for Rome?

> ARCHBISHOP MARCEL LEFEBVRE
> I am not sure, but I do want to be
> at our Holy Fathers funeral mass.

> DAKAR BISHOP
> Your Excellency do you need us to
> make visits for you?

> ARCHBISHOP MARCEL LEFEBVRE
> Yes, Please.

CUT TO:

POPE PIUS XII DIES

EXT. - DAY - FUNERAL MASS - OCTOBER 1958

The scene should be live footage of Pope Pius XII funeral mass. The scene will cut away with Archbishop Lefebrve watching the mass on Television in Dakar with his Bishops.

> ARCHBISHOP MARCEL LEFEBVRE
> Your Excellencies this is a pivotal
> period in Church History. You may
> be witnessing the end of the
> tradition as we know it.

> DAKAR BISHOP
> Your Excellency why would you say
> that?

(CONTINUED)

MARCEL: The Right Hand of God
CONTINUED:

> ARCHBISHOP MARCEL LEFEBVRE
> Let's say I have it from a reliable source and have seen some with my own eyes. The election of the next Pope will be one of the most important elections in Church History.

FADE OUT.

FADE IN:

ELECTION OF POPE JOHN XXIII

EXT - DAY - DAKAR CATHEDRAL - OCTOBER 28, 1959

The Archbishop is exiting the Cathedral after mass when he is approached by one of the Bishops.

> DAKAR BISHOP
> Your Excellency, they have elected a Pope. It is Cardinal Roncalli of Venice. Can you believe they would elect a Cardinal who is 77 years old?

> ARCHBISHOP MARCEL LEFEBVRE
> Yes. He will be a transitional Pope for sure. Did they say what his regnal name is?

> DAKAR BISHOP
> Yes. Pope John XXIII

> ARCHBISHOP MARCEL LEFEBVRE
> That was the name of the anti-pope!

> DAKAR BISHOP
> He said: " I chose John .. A name sweet to us because it is the name of our father, dear to me because it is the name of the humble parish church where I was baptized, the solemn name of numberless cathedrals scattered throughout the world, including our own basilica St. John Latern."

(CONTINUED)

MARCEL: The Right Hand of God
CONTINUED:

          ARCHBISHOP MARCEL LEFEBVRE
So by taking the name John XIII instead of the XIV he is affirming that Pope John XXIII was of antipapal status. How strange of a selection.

          DAKAR BISHOP
Are you leaving for Rome your Excellency?

          ARCHBISHOP MARCEL LEFEBVRE
I will await to be requested or summoned. Thank you your excellency for the information.

As the Archbishop walks away he talks to himself

          ARCHBISHOP MARCEL LEFEBVRE (CONT'D)
There you are! This will not last long. I will no doubt receive an invitation from Rome asking me to give up one position or the other. I truly don't care since it is God's will and not mine.

          FADE OUT.

FADE IN:

INT. - DAY - ARCHBISHOP LEFEBVRE DAKAR OFFICE - JUNE 1959

The scene opens with the Archbishop reading correspondence from Rome. His bags are packed and sitting along the side of his desk. In walks one of the Dakar Bishops.

          DAKAR BISHOP
Your Excellency, we will be leaving for our flight shortly. Do you need me to bring any of your bags to the car?

          ARCHBISHOP MARCEL LEFEBVRE
Yes thank you Pasquelae.

As he rises from his chair and heads to the door he says to Dakar Bishop.

          (CONTINUED)

MARCEL: The Right Hand of God
CONTINUED:

>   ARCHBISHOP MARCEL LEFEBVRE (CONT'D)
>   Well I received a letter from Rome
>   informing me that I have to choose
>   between remaining archbishop of
>   Dakar, therefore the Dakar Diocese
>   or apostolic delegate.
>
>   DAKAR BISHOP
>   Oh my Excellency how will you
>   respond?
>
>   ARCHBISHOP MARCEL LEFEBVRE
>   The only way I know how.
>
>   DAKAR BISHOP
>   That is?
>
>   ARCHBISHOP MARCEL LEFEBVRE
>   It is not up to me to chose because
>   I was not the one who appointed
>   myself to either office.
>   Consequently, I leave it up to the
>   authorities who made the
>   appointments; they must tell me if
>   I am to remain apostolic delegate
>   or rather archbishop of Dakar.
>
>   DAKAR BISHOP
>   How do you think they will respond?
>
>   ARCHBISHOP MARCEL LEFEBVRE
>   The only way they know how.
>
>   DAKAR BISHOP
>   How is that?
>
>   ARCHBISHOP MARCEL LEFEBVRE
>   The only way Rome knows how to
>   answer. By making it seem as though
>   I made the decision. They will say
>   something like *"Since you have
>   chosen to continue in the office of
>   archbishop of Dakar, you will
>   indeed remain archbishop and will
>   no longer be apostolic delegate"*
>
>   DAKAR BISHOP
>   I don't understand your Excellency,
>   have you not performed sufficiently
>   well as the apostolic delegate?
>   (MORE)

(CONTINUED)

MARCEL: The Right Hand of God
CONTINUED:

> DAKAR BISHOP (CONT'D)
> There has been great advancements under your direction.

> ARCHBISHOP MARCEL LEFEBVRE
> Pasquelae I have shielded you well from Rome. Your purity is refreshing. The Roman Curia is run by their own rules. It is not necessarily what is in the best interest of the Church as you and I are accustomed to, no, instead it is what is in the best interest of certain Bishops and Cardinals.

> DAKAR BISHOP
> So what will happen now?

> ARCHBISHOP MARCEL LEFEBVRE
> Well if in fact they take away my apostolic delegate position I will no longer have the responsibilities for all the dioceses. They will appoint a new apostolic delegate who will act in the manner they see fit. Almost certain I will lose my auxiliary, Bishop Guibert as well. They will most likely appoint him to a new location.

> DAKAR BISHOP
> Your Excellency is there anything I should be concerned with?

> ARCHBISHOP MARCEL LEFEBVRE
> Well I will still be Archbishop of Dakar but when the winds start blowing who knows what may change.

FADE OUT.

FADE IN:

> FR. WALTER JAEGER
> What did he mean, *"when the winds start blowing"*?

> FR. MICHAEL GABRIELLI
> Well Archbishop saw that after the war it became more clear much like the Holy Father was referring to.
> (MORE)

(CONTINUED)

MARCEL: The Right Hand of God
CONTINUED:

> FR. MICHAEL GABRIELLI (CONT'D)
> In the colonies, a wind of independence blew, generally coming from the United States, a political independence, economic independence and even religious independence that was favored by many members of the clergy and the Roman Curia. From a religious point of view, independence very simply meant replacing the European bishops with Afrian Bishops.

> FR. WALTER JAEGER
> Was that a bad thing? Why not African Bishops? We have American Bishops?

> FR. MICHAEL GABRIELLI
> If you knew Archbishop Lefebrve you would know he was never opposed to that. He was opposed to their formation. He was concerned that they were simply making them Bishops for political reasons. He was concerned they were not yet ready for such responsibilities. You see the same thing in the United States and Europe today. Those individuals not qualified but are promoted or positioned because of the politics. That is a very dangerous trend. Especially when it come to the Church.

> FR. WALTER JAEGER
> Oh I understand. Not qualified as opposed to ethnic background. What did do about it?

> FR. MICHAEL GABRIELLI
> Nothing much he could about it when as he said "*the winds start blowing*". Little by little he and the other bishops fully realized that they were becoming undesirables.

> FR. WALTER JAEGER
> What did Rome feel about it?

(CONTINUED)

MARCEL: The Right Hand of God
CONTINUED:

> **FR. MICHAEL GABRIELLI**
> It was also Rome's desire. Bishop Constantini made a remark at the Congregation of the Propaganda which shook Archbishop Lefebrve to his core about the matter.

> **FR. WALTER JAEGER**
> What was that?

> **FR. MICHAEL GABRIELLI**
> He said: *"If you think that it is the European bishops who are truly going to convert Africa and other mission countries, you are mistaken. There need to be African Bishops"*

> **FR. WALTER JAEGER**
> Well maybe because Bishop Constantini was not familiar with Africa he had slightly misplaced optimism?

> **FR. MICHAEL GABRIELLI**
> Said by a good disciple of Vatican II.

> **FR. WALTER JAEGER**
> Father I can't help being educated after vatican II. Why the barbs?

> **FR. MICHAEL GABRIELLI**
> Actually not a barb as much as making my point all together. See, the reason the archbishop was so overtaken by that statement is that he was not use to this type of dialogue from someone who had no clue about Africa. He was use to the Pope being the decision maker. He was use to having the conversation with the Pope on who was capable and not. The new was this new brand of committee thinking with out regard for what was best for the Church but rather how it would look.

> **FR. WALTER JAEGER**
> What was the archbishops response?

(CONTINUED)

MARCEL: The Right Hand of God
CONTINUED:

> FR. MICHAEL GABRIELLI
> He was very defensive because he knew how many decades it took to get Africa to the state it was in and didn't want Monday morning quarter backs, so to speak, influencing such a major decision. He responded the only way he knew. He said: "*Fine! Let there be African Bishops, BUT they also have to be capable; and they also have to have the means to continue the apostolate*"

> FR. WALTER JAEGER
> Seems right.

> FR. MICHAEL GABRIELLI
> He was right but at the same time he was getting a glimpse of what Pope Pius XII warned him against. Stay vigilant! Stay with the tradition! The archbishop was witnessing the new order, the new way, the new church of pansies and politicians. In short, the Liberals!

> FR. WALTER JAEGER
> So the times, they were a changing?
> (laughing)

> FR. MICHAEL GABRIELLI
> Very good Father! Yes, the times of thinking like Bob Dillion were at hand.

> FR. WALTER JAEGER
> What did the archbishop do?

> FR. MICHAEL GABRIELLI
> He fought the good fight as long as he could but eventually the Roman Curia began to push the obedience matter in his face and one thing archbishop Lefebvre always respected was obedience to his superiors. Later he would regret it.

(CONTINUED)

MARCEL: The Right Hand of God
   CONTINUED:

>   FR. WALTER JAEGER
>   Did he lose his archbishop
>   position?
>
>   FR. MICHAEL GABRIELLI
>   No. He waited until early 1962 when
>   the Second vatican Council was in
>   full bloom and he decided that
>   since he was part of the Councils
>   Preparatory Commission he would be
>   better serving the Church if he
>   kept his mind and attention on the
>   liberals at the council. So he
>   wrote a letter of resignation to
>   the Congregation of Propaganda.
>
>   FR. WALTER JAEGER
>   Did they accept? Did he have a
>   request for a transfer?
>
>   FR. MICHAEL GABRIELLI
>   He wrote: *"If you wish to put
>   someone else in my place. I would
>   be willing to hand in my
>   resignation and return to Europe. I
>   would have no problem with that"*
>
>   FR. WALTER JAEGER
>   And there response?
>
>   FR. MICHAEL GABRIELLI
>   *"Fine, we accept your resignation.
>   You will go back to Europe"*
>
>   FR. WALTER JAEGER
>   So that worked out?
>
>   FR. MICHAEL GABRIELLI
>   Well, he asked that they wait at
>   least 6 months before reappointing
>   him elsewhere. He actually was
>   waiting for the Holy Ghost Fathers
>   General Chapter in August, 1962. He
>   also thought there was a good
>   possibility to become the Superior
>   General of The Holy Ghost Fathers.
>   He actually had an interest to get
>   involved with the English-Speaking
>   territories and perfect his
>   english.

                                                        (CONTINUED)

MARCEL: The Right Hand of God
CONTINUED:

> FR. WALTER JAEGER
> How did they respond?

> FR. MICHAEL GABRIELLI
> "*No, No, it is out of the question. You must be a bishop in France!*"

> FR. WALTER JAEGER
> Well that seems to make sense. He was French, he spent his entire vocation in French governed countries. Am I missing something?

> FR. MICHAEL GABRIELLI
> Yes. He knew the Bishops in France thought of him. They were afraid of him because he was a Traditionalist or integrist. Even then, even before Vatican II was finalized.

> FR. WALTER JAEGER
> If they feared him then, what would the bishops due now?

> FR. MICHAEL GABRIELLI
> Exactly what they are doing to the Society of Pius X now.

> FR. WALTER JAEGER
> What was the reason for their fear? He was almost exclusively in Africa.

> FR. MICHAEL GABRIELLI
> Well, he often visited a group founded by Jean Ousset called "*La Cite Catholique*" one day while the archbishop was still in Dakar the Prior of Solesmes sent him a letter.

CUT TO:

INT. - NIGHT - ARCHBISHOP LEFEBVRES DAKAR COURTYARD - 1955

This flashback scene opens with the archbishop sitting on a bench in the Dakar Courtyard reading a letter from Jean Ousset. The view will be of the letter as he reads it in a narrative voice.

(CONTINUED)

MARCEL: The Right Hand of God
CONTINUED:

> ARCHBISHOP MARCEL LEFEBVRE
> "Your excellency you should support these good people. They are very courageous; they have a strong faith; they are militant and are trying hard to make contacts with the bishops. The bishops are wary of them though, and so they are not really very supportive. You would do them a service if you went to see them, said that you are in agreement with them, and that you will help their movement to restore Catholic principles."

A Dakar Bishop walks up to speak to the archbishop.

> DAKAR BISHOP
> Your Excellency you asked for me?

> ARCHBISHOP MARCEL LEFEBVRE
> Yes. Are you familiar with a group founded by Jean Ousset in France called Cité catholique?

> DAKAR BISHOP
> Some what.

> ARCHBISHOP MARCEL LEFEBVRE
> What and who are they?

> DAKAR BISHOP
> Following the Liberation of France, Cité catholique, a Catholic fundamentalist group started to take hold.

> ARCHBISHOP MARCEL LEFEBVRE
> What are their aims and goals?

> DAKAR BISHOP
> As the Cagoule had done before the war, the Cité catholique have as their aim to encourage the Republic's elites in order to form a National Catholic state.
> (MORE)

(CONTINUED)

MARCEL: The Right Hand of God
CONTINUED:

> DAKAR BISHOP (CONT'D)
> Their fear is that France has become too liberal and too modernistic, that it has lost its position as a country that was once the daughter of the Church.

> ARCHBISHOP MARCEL LEFEBVRE
> What about it's founder Jean Ousset, what do you know of him?

> DAKAR BISHOP
> Jean Ousset, their founder wrote *Le Marxisme-Léninisme* in which he argued that Marxists could only be combatted by "a profound faith, an unlimited obedience to the Holy Father, and a thorough knowledge of the Church's doctrines."

> ARCHBISHOP MARCEL LEFEBVRE
> A Traditionalist?

> DAKAR BISHOP
> Yes, but as you know France now, anyone who is devoted to the Church is considered in direct rebellion with the Government. They are getting a lot of bad press.

> ARCHBISHOP MARCEL LEFEBVRE
> What support are they getting from the Church?

> DAKAR BISHOP
> Little to none. The Bishops of France are afraid of them or I should say the government if they knew they were supporting their efforts.

> ARCHBISHOP MARCEL LEFEBVRE
> That would explain this letter I received.

> DAKAR BISHOP
> So will you make contact with them?

(CONTINUED)

MARCEL: The Right Hand of God
CONTINUED:

> ARCHBISHOP MARCEL LEFEBVRE
> How can I refuse?

FADE OUT.

FADE IN:

> FR. WALTER JAEGER
> So that is why the French Bishops feared him?

> FR. MICHAEL GABRIELLI
> He met with Jean Ousset and then Cité catholique published the book "*Pour Qu'Il Regne*" whiuch was their charter. They asked the archbishop to write a preface and he did.

> FR. WALTER JAEGER
> What kind of book was it?

> FR. MICHAEL GABRIELLI
> Excellent book. You should read it. A book of faith in Christendom, in Our Lord in the social kingship of Our Lord.

> FR. WALTER JAEGER
> So what was the outcome?

> FR. MICHAEL GABRIELLI
> The Bishops of France were against the movement and once they heard of the Archbishops affiliation with the group and the book they said "*That's it! Archbishop Lefebvre has to interfere with our business again by writing a letter for "La Cite Catholique"*"

> FR. WALTER JAEGER
> So if he was transferred to France as a Bishop he would be in a very uncomfortable position.

> FR. MICHAEL GABRIELLI
> Well Pope John XXIII insisted that he become a Bishop of France and met with the French Bishops to make it so. But the Bishops gave the Pope conditions.

(CONTINUED)

MARCEL: The Right Hand of God
CONTINUED:

> FR. WALTER JAEGER
> What conditions?

> FR. MICHAEL GABRIELLI
> 1. That he not be a member of the Assembly of Cardinals and Archbishops
>
> 2. That he have only a small diocese and not an archdiocese.
>
> 3. That this not be considered a precedent.

> FR. WALTER JAEGER
> As so that is how he became the Bishop of Tulle. Wasn't that a demotion of sorts?

> FR. MICHAEL GABRIELLI
> Of course. It showed the vindictiveness of the French Bishops. They knew very well of all his great accomplishments as an archbishop of Africa. But the Archbishop handled it with the utmost humility. He simply accepted and said to the Holy Father. " A small diocese is fine and to borrow a sentence of St. Francis de Sales' A single soul is a large diocese" Well I have 225,000 souls and that makes it a great diocese."

> FR. WALTER JAEGER
> But I thought he became the Superior General of The Holy Ghost Fathers in 1962.

> FR. MICHAEL GABRIELLI
> You are correct. He was not the Bishop of Tulle very long. In that same year, August 1962 he was elected as the Superior General of the Holy Ghost Fathers. The Second Vatican Council officially opened in October, 1962. But his election was eventful as well.

CUT TO:

MARCEL: The Right Hand of God

LEFEBVRE BECOMES SUPERIOR GENERAL

INT. - NIGHT - CHEVILLY-LARUE - AUGUST 22, 1962

The scene open with a large conference room at the General Chapter House in Chevilly-Larue with many religious at the table. A bishop stands up and prepares the delegation for the election.

> BISHOP AUGNIBENI
> As you all know we need a 2/3rds vote is required. A Bishop can not be elected Superior General with only a simple majority. 51% is not good enough, there must be 67%. We will begin balloting, do you understand?

> GROUP ASSEMBLED
> Yes!

> BISHOP AUGNIBENI
> Okay we will pass out the Ballots and begin the election.

The scene shows the room they are gathered and then a shot of the clock that moves from 8:00 to 8:15. Then back to Fr. Augnibeni.

> BISHOP AUGNIBENI (CONT'D)
> We have the following votes: 65% Bishop Lefebvre; 20% Bishop Turlo; 10% Bishop Voigt and 5% Bishop Viola. I am sorry that we could not have a 67% majority vote so we will have to start the balloting over again.

> HOLY GHOST BISHOP
> Your Excellency, with all due respect, why are we wasting any more time. It is clear by the voting that Bishop Lefebvre is clearly elected since Bishop Turlo is 45% behind. Do you expect to keep voting until we reach 67%?

> BISHOP AUGNIBENI
> We must have a 2/3rd's majority. These are our rules.

(CONTINUED)

MARCEL: The Right Hand of God
CONTINUED:

> ARCHBISHOP MARCEL LEFEBVRE
> Listen, for goodness sake, let me stay in the diocese of Tulle. I arrived there six months ago; I am beginning to know the priests, the people, the works of the diocese. For two years they were without a bishop. Will they again be left without a bishop? Since Pope John XXIII appointed me to the diocese of Tulle, leave me there.

> BISHOP TURLO
> Your Excellency, I understand but Bishop Augnibeni is right. The rules call for 2/3rds and we must continue.

> ARCHBISHOP MARCEL LEFEBVRE
> Then continue we will!

The scene shows the a shot of the clock that moves from 8:30 to 8:45. Then back to Fr. Augnibeni.

> BISHOP AUGNIBENI
> We have the following votes: 72% Bishop Lefebvre; 10% Bishop Turlo; 10% Bishop Voigt and 8% Bishop Viola. It appears Bishop Lefebvre is our new Superior General. I would like to be the first to congratulate your Excellency because I know of no other who has done more for the Holy Ghost Fathers.

All the attendee's stand up to applaud the election as Bishop Lefebvre slowly rises from his chair with a slightly blushed smile on his faith acknowledging his acceptance and appreciation. As Bishop Lefebrve walks around the room for several minutes he walks up to Bishop Augnibeni.

> ARCHBISHOP MARCEL LEFEBVRE
> Your Excellency we still need the Pope's approbation. Our election and the decision of the Holy Ghost Fathers does not have the authority to remove me as the Bishop of Tulle.

(CONTINUED)

MARCEL: The Right Hand of God
CONTINUED:

> BISHOP AUGNIBENI
> I am a step ahead of you Marcel. The General Secretary has already sent a telegram to Rome which read *"Confirmation requested for the election of Bishop Lefebvre as superior general of the Holy Ghost Fathers"*

> ARCHBISHOP MARCEL LEFEBVRE
> Very good. I will await his response.

> BISHOP AUGNIBENI
> Well not to disappoint you but we must have had perfect timing because we already received his response.

> ARCHBISHOP MARCEL LEFEBVRE
> And?

> BISHOP AUGNIBENI
> His answer was *"I bless the election of Archbishop Lefebvre, superior general of the Holy Ghost Fathers"*

> ARCHBISHOP MARCEL LEFEBVRE
> There you have it.

> BISHOP AUGNIBENI
> You are once again all ours. All 5,200 members and 60 Bishops Congratulations.

> ARCHBISHOP MARCEL LEFEBVRE
> Do you know what is so interesting about our order?

> BISHOP AUGNIBENI
> We have a rich history of serving the poor and marginalized?

> ARCHBISHOP MARCEL LEFEBVRE
> Close. Most people do not know that we are the order of the Black people. Where ever there are Africans there we are. Whether it is Harlem, New York or New Orleans or Gabon we are there.
> (MORE)

(CONTINUED)

MARCEL: The Right Hand of God
CONTINUED:

> ARCHBISHOP MARCEL LEFEBVRE (CONT'D)
> Most people do not know that in the 1840s our order was dedicated to working with newly freed slaves on the islands of Haiti, Mauritius and Réunion.

> BISHOP AUGNIBENI
> What is even more fascinating is that our founder Fr. Francis Libermann, our first superior general was a Jewish convert.

> ARCHBISHOP MARCEL LEFEBVRE
> Now I will take over as Superior General just as the Council is about to open.

FADE OUT.

FADE IN:

> FR. WALTER JAEGER
> So Father his order must have known how good of a Archbishop he was to have such a large approval at the election.

> FR. MICHAEL GABRIELLI
> He did more for the advancement of the order than any before him. They knew he was a great man.

> FR. WALTER JAEGER
> What about the Second Vatican Council?

> FR. MICHAEL GABRIELLI
> It was a time of great confusion and change. The council was opened to let fresh air into the Church but it was never meant to be a pastoral council. But once the liberals got a hold it, the winds starting blowing very hard and fast.

> FR. WALTER JAEGER
> In what way?

(CONTINUED)

MARCEL: The Right Hand of God
CONTINUED:

>   FR. MICHAEL GABRIELLI
>   At first, when Pope John XXIII
>   began the council there were many
>   meetings, committees, many
>   discussions. But the Archbishop
>   felt that the council should have
>   been closed before the death of
>   John XXIII, but no that would not
>   be the case.

                                                    CUT TO:

POPE JOHN XXIII DIES

INT. - NIGHT - HOLY GHOST MOTHERHOUSE - RUE LHOMOND - 1963

The scene is the Archbishop having a conversation with a priest from Duquesne University, Pittsburgh when a Bishop rushes into the room to inform the Archbishop of Pope John XXIII death.

>   HOLY GHOST BISHOP
>   Your Excellency, please excuse my
>   interruption!
>
>   ARCHBISHOP MARCEL LEFEBVRE
>   Yes? What is it?
>
>   HOLY GHOST BISHOP
>   Our Holy Father has died!
>
>   HOLY GHOST PRIEST
>   Your Excellency, I will make my
>   leave as you must have much more
>   important matters to attend to now.

The Archbishop ignores the priests request and addresses the Bishop?

>   ARCHBISHOP MARCEL LEFEBVRE
>   When? When did he die?
>
>   HOLY GHOST BISHOP
>   This morning your Excellency.

Then the Archbishop looks over to the priest and addresses him almost as if he is still thinking about the information he just received.

                                                (CONTINUED)

MARCEL: The Right Hand of God
CONTINUED:

> **ARCHBISHOP MARCEL LEFEBVRE**
> No father please stay. If I am requested to leave for Rome I will do so. As for now much will be done for his funeral preparation and then the college of Cardinals will convene.

The Bishop leaves the room and leaves the Archbishop and Priest to continue with their discussions.

> **HOLY GHOST PRIEST**
> Your Excellency how terrible, how terrible that our Holy Father was not able to finalize the Council before his death.

> **ARCHBISHOP MARCEL LEFEBVRE**
> Father, throughout my involvement I will tell you that this council may last for quite a while. Not a good thing.

> **HOLY GHOST PRIEST**
> Why your Excellency?

> **ARCHBISHOP MARCEL LEFEBVRE**
> I truly don't think they know what they are trying to achieve. It is as if anything is open for discussion and anything possible. Way too many liberal ideas floating through these committees. Certain Bishops and Cardinals including me are asked to be involved in these committees and just when we submit our work after months and years, we get a polite slap on the back and they completely disregard our recommendations. It is as if we are part of a sham.

> **HOLY GHOST PRIEST**
> A sham your Excellency?

(CONTINUED)

MARCEL: The Right Hand of God
CONTINUED:

>   ARCHBISHOP MARCEL LEFEBVRE
>   Yes. As Pope Pius XXII told me, be
>   careful of those that push for a
>   new council because their
>   intentions are anything but
>   spiritual, anything but of Christ
>   our King and Mother Church. He was
>   so right and now I understand why
>   he fought this council.
>
>   HOLY GHOST PRIEST
>   What do you see will happen now?
>
>   ARCHBISHOP MARCEL LEFEBVRE
>   Truthfully Father, I fear the next
>   Papal selection because the liberal
>   power and positions are so
>   influential that it may be a Pope
>   who will allow these matters to get
>   even further adrift.

                                                    FADE OUT.

ELECTION OF POPE PAUL VI

FADE IN:

EXT - NIGHT - VATICAN SQUARE - 1963

A news reporter is seen covering the progress of the College of Cardinals while standing in the Vatican Square among all the people gathered as Archbishop follows along through the TV coverage back in France.

>   CBS NEWS REPORTER
>   We have been waiting for 2 days for
>   the election of the new Pontiff of
>   the Catholic Church. Pope John
>   XXIII was considered a transitional
>   Pope but many came to love him as a
>   Grandfather figure as well. Truly
>   he was Happy and Jolly John and
>   loved by both Catholics and non-
>   Catholics.

White spoke can be seen coming from the Cistine Chapel Chimney as a cheer goes up and the crowd roar with excitement. The reporter stops in mid stream and changes his discussion.

(CONTINUED)

MARCEL: The Right Hand of God
CONTINUED:

> CBS NEWS REPORTER (CONT'D)
> Wait! It looks as if we have a new
> Pope. The ____ Pope! We will wait
> to hear who the new Pope is and
> what name he takes.

The Archbishop is sitting in the TV room at the Holy Ghost Mother House in Paris when discussions start to breakout.

> HOLY GHOST BISHOP
> Your Excellency, who do you think
> it will be?

> ARCHBISHOP MARCEL LEFEBVRE
> I have no clue but I have heard
> Cardinal Sarto is very popular
> among the Curia. That would be an
> excellent choice.

> HOLY GHOST BISHOP
> Wasn't our Holy Father very
> favorable to Cardinal Montinni?

> ARCHBISHOP MARCEL LEFEBVRE
> He was and that could be very
> difficult for the Church.

The news reporter starts to deliver the news again.

> CBS NEWS REPORTER
> The new Pope is Cardinal Montinni
> of Millan!

> ARCHBISHOP MARCEL LEFEBVRE
> There you have it. Hold on because
> the Council will continue! Oh well
> back to the business of Superior
> General.

FADE OUT.

FADE IN:

> FR. WALTER JAEGER
> How long did he remain the Superior
> General?

> FR. MICHAEL GABRIELLI
> From 1962 to 1968.

(CONTINUED)

MARCEL: The Right Hand of God
CONTINUED:

> **FR. WALTER JAEGER**
> Only 6 years? That was a short term. Not typical.

> **FR. MICHAEL GABRIELLI**
> After the council had closed, Pope Paul VI asked all the religious congregations to hold an extraordinary General Chapter in order to adapt their constitutions to the spirit of the Second Vatican Council. That was pretty much the end of the line for the Archbishop.

> **FR. WALTER JAEGER**
> Why was that a problem?

> **FR. MICHAEL GABRIELLI**
> It was very vague, very difficult and very dangerous and it brought with it a deterioration of authority in the Holy Ghost order. The Archbishop's term was suppose to last until 1974 but he decided to have a vote in order to see if the Superior General's authority was even required due to the changes brought about by the Council.

CUT TO:

INT. - DAY - MONTE MARIO, ROME HOLY GHOST MOTHERHOUSE - 1968

The scene opens with Archbishop walking through the courtyard reading his breviary. The Archbishop's brother Rene arrived at the Mother house for a surprise visit.

> **FR. RENE LEFEBVRE**
> My Brother looks so regal and yet so spiritual.

> **ARCHBISHOP MARCEL LEFEBVRE**
> Rene! I didn't know you were coming to Rome! Why didn't you call ahead?

As he rushes to embrace his brother.

(CONTINUED)

MARCEL: The Right Hand of God
CONTINUED:

> ARCHBISHOP MARCEL LEFEBVRE (CONT'D)
> You are a sight for sore eye's - how good to have you hear.

> FR. RENE LEFEBVRE
> Marcel you seem to be so very busy and I thought the only way to get any time with you was to just drop in. Of course your secretary kept me posted on your plans (laughing).

> ARCHBISHOP MARCEL LEFEBVRE
> I understand you have asked to retire? You know Lefebvre's never retire, we just fade away.

> FR. RENE LEFEBVRE
> Well there is some truth to it. It is time for the younger Priests to take over for us old folk.

> ARCHBISHOP MARCEL LEFEBVRE
> Based on what I have seen come out of the council and the goings on in the order I am not so sure about that. I think our work may have just begun.

> FR. RENE LEFEBVRE
> Brother the times are changing, you know that. The African's are now positioned to taken over the Church and we have done what was required of us. As for the priest in other parts of the world I am somewhat out of touch. What is going on?

> ARCHBISHOP MARCEL LEFEBVRE
> It seems we have lost the need for our own constitutions. Some of the members of General Chapter, especially the Dutch, manifested their desire that our constitutions no longer be enforced.

> FR. RENE LEFEBVRE
> Well doesn't the Congregation for Religious have a say about that?

(CONTINUED)

MARCEL: The Right Hand of God
CONTINUED:

> ARCHBISHOP MARCEL LEFEBVRE
> Even without any authorization from the Congregation for Religious, they wanted the Chapter to be presided over by a triumvirate.

> FR. RENE LEFEBVRE
> But you are the Superior General, surely you have some say, some influence? I thought it was written in the constitution that the Superior General would direct all the business of the General Chapter?

> ARCHBISHOP MARCEL LEFEBVRE
> You would think! But I tell you Rene this fever that came out of the Second Vatican Council is taking hold over everything and everybody. It is like everyone has gone mad.

> FR. RENE LEFEBVRE
> Who is leading this movement?

> ARCHBISHOP MARCEL LEFEBVRE
> That is what is so perplexing. It is a small minority. Are you familiar with Fr. Lecuyer the professor at the seminary here in Rome?

> FR. RENE LEFEBVRE
> No very well. I have heard his name before.

> ARCHBISHOP MARCEL LEFEBVRE
> He is one of them. They absolutely hate the tradition. They want a reformation the likes of Martin Luther. But I tell you even Martin Luther would blush at their plans of reform. Fr. Le Froch would be horrified if he were around to witness this.

> FR. RENE LEFEBVRE
> What are your plans?

(CONTINUED)

MARCEL: The Right Hand of God
CONTINUED:

> ARCHBISHOP MARCEL LEFEBVRE
> Rene I have no choice but to see if my authority is even in place anymore. I am going to call a meeting of the Chapter.

> FR. RENE LEFEBVRE
> My God I had no clue it was that bad. What will you do if they decide you are no longer needed?

> ARCHBISHOP MARCEL LEFEBVRE
> God only knows. Maybe it is my time as well to retire. But I keep hearing the haunting words of Fr. Le Froch, our Father and Pope Pius XII to stay vigilant, stay vigilant!

> FR. RENE LEFEBVRE
> At what cost Marcel?

> ARCHBISHOP MARCEL LEFEBVRE
> What cost did our Father pay? At what cost? The ultimate cost!

> FR. RENE LEFEBVRE
> Marcel maybe you are not looking at this the right way.

Rene stops and puts himself in check before proceeding.

> FR. RENE LEFEBVRE (CONT'D)
> Never mind my Brother. You have done so much for the order and seen so much more than I, I have no right to advise you on this matter.

> ARCHBISHOP MARCEL LEFEBVRE
> Well Rene, I have been very fortunate due to Divine Providence. I feel as if before all my tests were on behalf of the faith and the church. I only had to deal with pagan cultures and political and governmental oversight type battles. Now I feel I am battling with the real devil and that devil is inside our own church.

(CONTINUED)

MARCEL: The Right Hand of God
CONTINUED:

> **FR RENE LEFEBRVE**
> I guess I am just ignorant to all the goings on.

> **ARCHBISHOP MARCEL LEFEBVRE**
> When the council was in full bloom and I was part of the Congregations trying to understand the basis of the council, I was walking to a meeting when a young Priest came up to me and provided me with a book called "*The Plot Against the Church*" written by Maurice Pinay and 12 other Priests. It was a real eye opener. Have you read it?

> **FR. RENE LEFEBVRE**
> No!

> **ARCHBISHOP MARCEL LEFEBVRE**
> There truly is a conspiracy against our Mother Church. Why in the world would our Holy Father have so many Protestant leaders involved in the council. This is under heard of and is quite heretical.

> **FR. RENE LEFEBVRE**
> You are sounding like our Father now.

> **ARCHBISHOP MARCEL LEFEBVRE**
> Yes! Father saw so much, and he always cautioned us about it. Now it has arrived. What shall I do? Run away and hide? No I will not run! I will stay and fight!

CUT TO:

LEFEBVRE RESIGNS AS SUPERIOR GENERAL

INT. - DAY - GENERAL CHAPTER MEETING - ROME 1968

The scene opens similar to the opening of the Superior General election. Many Bishops are gathers and priest are allowed to sit in to listen. The Archbishop rises from his chair to address the congregation.

(CONTINUED)

MARCEL: The Right Hand of God
CONTINUED:

> ARCHBISHOP MARCEL LEFEBVRE
> Thank you all for coming to this
> emergency Chapter Meeting. I would
> like to start with the Angelus.

The Archbishop starts the Angelus with a weak response other than the Bishops. Certain Priest are viewed as being disinterested in the prayer and eager for the meeting. After the prayer the Archbishop begins the discussion.

> ARCHBISHOP MARCEL LEFEBVRE (CONT'D)
> It has come to my attention that
> many in the order are prescribing
> that a triumvirate be elected and
> there be an elimination of the
> Superior general position in which
> I currently hold. Although I feel
> this is completely against the
> constitution of our order and
> should first be approved by myself
> and the Congregation of Religious.

The Archbishop eyes Fr. Lecuyer who is listening intently but looks away with embarrassment when he notices the Archbishop looking directly at him. But then gains his composure and returns a stern disobedient look.

> ARCHBISHOP MARCEL LEFEBVRE (CONT'D)
> However, if it be the wish of the
> General Chapter that I step down
> and that the Superior General
> position be eliminated I will leave
> it to that. We will have a vote and
> which ever way the vote goes I will
> be in agreement.

The group of Bishops all huddle together and begin their discussions. The Archbishop walks out of the room, his age starting to show in his walk. A shot of a clock on the wall shows the time pass from 1:00 p.m. To 3:00 p.m. (to represent the time of the crucifixion of Christ). The scene returns with Bishop Augnibeni walking up to the Archbishop with the results of the balloting. The Archbishop reads the results and gestures for the Bishop to read the results.

> BISHOP AUGNIBENI
> The Superior General has asked me
> to read the results of the
> balloting. The majority vote is to
> eliminate the position of Superior
> General.

(CONTINUED)

MARCEL: The Right Hand of God
CONTINUED:

A loud cheer goes up in the room lead by Fr. Lecuyer and as the Archbishop looks at him he returns a stern and disrespectful smile. Other bishops are viewed with great remorse and concern on their faces, but the Archbishop simply rises and once again proceeds to leave the room.

          BISHOP AUGNIBENI (CONT'D)
     There will be a separate Chapter
     Meeting to elect 3 priests to the
     Triumvirate. We will inform
     everyone of this meeting date and
     time.

At that Bishop Augnibeni turns around to look at the Archbishop and discovers he has left the room. The Bishop hurries to catch up with the Archbishop.

          BISHOP AUGNIBENI (CONT'D)
     Your Excellency wait! You must sign
     all the proceedings in order to
     make them official. Wait!

The Archbishop stops and slowly turns around to face the Bishop almost as Christ would have turned to face St. Peter.

          ARCHBISHOP MARCEL LEFEBVRE
     Your Excellency is it not enough
     that I must witness everything
     being turned upside down,
     completely changed and that the
     Congregation of my most beloved
     order to adopt a new spirit, a
     spirit which I can not let into my
     order? This spirit which I fought
     so sternly against during the
     council proceedings?

          BISHOP AUGNIBENI
     Your Excellency, your fights and
     battles during the Council are well
     known. It is for that very fact
     that we find ourselves at this
     point.

(CONTINUED)

MARCEL: The Right Hand of God
CONTINUED:

                    ARCHBISHOP MARCEL LEFEBVRE
        This point! This point! You ask me
        to sign all these proceedings which
        in reality would sanction the
        Congregations destruction, and that
        in the Congregations history it
        would be said that "Archbishop
        Lefebvre was the one who,
        practically speaking, by his
        signature, was responsible for it.
        That I can not and will not accept
        your Excellency! Never!

                    BISHOP AUGNIBENI
        But your Excellency .....

Bishop Augnibeni suddenly realized what he himself was a part of and what damage could be laid at his feet. He looks at the Archbishop with remorse and simply bends to his right knee and kisses his ring.

                    BISHOP AUGNIBENI (CONT'D)
        God bless you your Excellency. You
        truly are the right hand of God.

Bishop Augnibeni turns around and slowly returns to the room that is full of laughter and joyous celebration. There is a close up of Archbishop Lefebrve and he has a flash back to his childhood when he is visiting his mother in Jail and she speaks these soft words to him.

                    GABRIELLE LEFEBRVE
        Marcel, do not cry. When you are
        doing what is right you only need
        to place yourself in the bosom of
        the Blessed Mother and all will be
        fine. We are not of this world but
        only in it. Stand firm, Stand fast!

                                  FADE OUT.

FADE IN:

INT. - DAY - LITHUANIAN HOUSE - ROME - 1968

Archbishop is in the commissary of the Lithuanian House having lunch being tended to by the German Sisters of St. Catherine when his brother Rene rushes into the room looking disheveled. He approaches the Archbishop.

MARCEL: The Right Hand of God
CONTINUED:

>   FR. RENE LEFEBVRE
> Marcel! There you are! I have been
> looking all over Rome for you. What
> Happened!

>   ARCHBISHOP MARCEL LEFEBVRE
> It's over Rene. My time has come to
> an end.

>   FR RENE LEFEBRVE
> What are you talking about? What
> are you doing here?

>   ARCHBISHOP MARCEL LEFEBVRE
> I am sure you know I stepped down
> as Superior General?

>   FR RENE LEFEBRVE
> Yes, I heard and I am sorry I could
> not attend the Chapter meeting.
> Honesty I didn't even receive an
> invitation to join.

>   ARCHBISHOP MARCEL LEFEBVRE
> That was for the better. It was a
> terrible assembly. I didn't resign
> as much as I was voted out. Its the
> new way, the new order of things
> due to the council. The order will
> be run by 3 priests.

>   FR. RENE LEFEBVRE
> Marcel it is the new way, we are
> the past.

>   ARCHBISHOP MARCEL LEFEBVRE
> Prior to the meeting I went to see
> Cardinal Antoniutti at the
> Congregation for Religious.

>   FR. RENE LEFEBVRE
> And?

>   ARCHBISHOP MARCEL LEFEBVRE
> He was visiting South America at
> the time and so I was asked to meet
> with the Congregation Secretary. So
> I explained the situation.

>   FR RENE LEFEBRVE
> And?

(CONTINUED)

MARCEL: The Right Hand of God
CONTINUED:

> ARCHBISHOP MARCEL LEFEBVRE
> So I explained the situation within the order and asked "Are you, or are you not, in agreement with all of this?" The response I received was "Oh, you know since the Council, you have to understand how it is. In fact, you see, the superior of the Redemptorist Congregation just came for the same reason"

> FR. RENE LEFEBVRE
> Your kidding? So this is happening across the other religious orders?

> ARCHBISHOP MARCEL LEFEBVRE
> I am afraid so.

> FR RENE LEFEBRVE
> Then what did the Secretary say?

> ARCHBISHOP MARCEL LEFEBVRE
> He advised me the same way he did the Redemptorist Superior General.

> FR. RENE LEFEBVRE
> And that was?

> ARCHBISHOP MARCEL LEFEBVRE
> To take a trip to America.

> FR. RENE LEFEBVRE
> America? Why America? Is that code for something?

> ARCHBISHOP MARCEL LEFEBVRE
> Who knows. I said, I am not going to America and abandon my Congregation on such a pivotal issue. I then left and decided to write to the Pope himself and present my resignation.

> FR. RENE LEFEBVRE
> And what did the Pope reply?

> ARCHBISHOP MARCEL LEFEBVRE
> He simply accepted it. As if this was the plan all along. Nothing more.
> (MORE)

(CONTINUED)

MARCEL: The Right Hand of God
CONTINUED:

> **ARCHBISHOP MARCEL LEFEBVRE (CONT'D)**
> Nothing about the past successes and achievements under Pope Pius XII. As cardinal Montinni was very close to Pius XII he knew quite well. Oh well.

> **FR. RENE LEFEBVRE**
> This unbelievable to me. Brother we have been through 2 world wars and yet this seems crazier than those days.

> **ARCHBISHOP MARCEL LEFEBVRE**
> Rene I tell you that this is the 3rd World War. The first two killed millions of people, but this War, this Vatican II will claim millions and millions of souls. This is a Spiritual war!

> **FR. RENE LEFEBVRE**
> I never thought the world could see anything worse than the like of Hitler and Stalin.

> **ARCHBISHOP MARCEL LEFEBVRE**
> I tell you Rene, do you remember how a fog came over Europe and the Urals as both Stalin and Hitler came to power?

> **FR. RENE LEFEBVRE**
> I do, it was a very eerie time and feeling.

> **ARCHBISHOP MARCEL LEFEBVRE**
> Do you remember how everyone used the terms in those days that it was a different time and we need to be patient. That Hitler wasn't that bad? Do you remember the support the German people and Russian people gave these demons?

> **FR. RENE LEFEBVRE**
> I sure do. Our father was one of those victims.

> **ARCHBISHOP MARCEL LEFEBVRE**
> No! We were all one of those victims. This council is the same.
> (MORE)

(CONTINUED)

MARCEL: The Right Hand of God
CONTINUED:

ARCHBISHOP MARCEL LEFEBVRE (CONT'D)
Everyone seems to be acting the very same way. If you stand up against anything they attack you the same way they did that many years ago. It is as if everyone is in a haze, drinking the same wine and being intoxicated with this liberal, humanistic, ecumenical nonsense. Just the same. They even have the same look in their eyes as they did back then.

FR RENE LEFEBRVE
Marcel you can't even compare the two.

ARCHBISHOP MARCEL LEFEBVRE
Oh yes I can. This is the 3rd World War. The first two killed millions of people, but this War, this Vatican II will claim millions and millions of souls. This is a Spiritual war - much, much worse!

FR. RENE LEFEBVRE
Well what brought you to the Lithuanian House? Are you considering joining their order?

ARCHBISHOP MARCEL LEFEBVRE
No. I just needed somewhere to stay and they took me in. They are very kind and very devote.

FR. RENE LEFEBVRE
What will you do next?

ARCHBISHOP MARCEL LEFEBVRE
The Congregation of the Propaganda asked me to work for them and take charge of African catechism project.

FR. RENE LEFEBVRE
Will you go?

ARCHBISHOP MARCEL LEFEBVRE
Yes for now but not for long. This new catechism will soon end all that as well.
(MORE)

(CONTINUED)

MARCEL: The Right Hand of God
CONTINUED:

> ARCHBISHOP MARCEL LEFEBVRE (CONT'D)
> I will take some time to let our
> Lord tell me what he wants of me
> next. I have learned never to
> precede providence.

FADE OUT.

FADE IN:

THE TRADITIONAL SOCIETY BEGINS

INT. - DAY - LITHUANIAN HOUSE - ROME - 1969

The Archbishop is sitting in the library of the Lithuanian House when a Sister walks in to inform him that he had visitors from the French Seminary in Rome have come to see him.

> SISTER GABRIELLA MARIE
> Your Excellency you have 6 visitors
> from the French Seminary to see
> you.

> ARCHBISHOP MARCEL LEFEBVRE
> Who are they Sister?

> SISTER GABRIELLA MARIE
> Clerics your Excellency.

> ARCHBISHOP MARCEL LEFEBVRE
> Do you know what they want to meet
> me about?

> SISTER GABRIELLA MARIE
> I am not sure but they look very
> determined to speak with you, your
> Excellency.

> ARCHBISHOP MARCEL LEFEBVRE
> Hmmm Determined Clerics hey?
> (laughing) Okay please send them
> in.

> SISTER GABRIELLA MARIE
> Very good your Excellency.

(CONTINUED)

MARCEL: The Right Hand of God
CONTINUED:

The clerics all shuffled into the room with much concern on their face and somewhat apprehensive on who will begin to speak and how to ask the Archbishop what they came to meet with him about. One by one they approach the Archbishop and drop to their right knee to kiss his Bishops ring.

> ARCHBISHOP MARCEL LEFEBVRE
> Yes, how can I help you?

> CLERIC AULAGNIER
> Your Excellency, please excuse us barging in on you like this but we need your help.

> CLERIC COTTARD
> Yes we were told you above all would understand our problem.

> ARCHBISHOP MARCEL LEFEBVRE
> Okay, what is your problem? How can I help you?

> CLERIC AULAGNIER
> Your Excellency we are all seminarians at the French Seminary here in Rome. The seminary situation is going from bad to worse.

> ARCHBISHOP MARCEL LEFEBVRE
> I can only imagine. I think I know of your problems already.

> CLERIC COTTARD
> Your Excellency there are is no more discipline. The Seminarians are going out at night, no cassocks, weekly liturgical changes.

> CLERIC AULAGNIER
> Yes, they have a liturgical group in charge who are making up new liturgy every week. There is incredible disorder and seems as if those in charge are doing all to discourage us from remaining. They don't want to provide a proper formation as they do a group of hip guys.

(CONTINUED)

MARCEL: The Right Hand of God
CONTINUED:

> **ARCHBISHOP MARCEL LEFEBVRE**
> Such a shame. I had such a great formation in the French Seminary under Fr. Le Froch. I can't tell you I don't know about what you are telling me. It is no surprise. But, what can I do about it? I am no longer in a position to do anything to change your situation.

> **CLERIC AULAGNIER**
> That is exactly why we came to see you. We know you have no commitments and we have turned to others and have been turned away every time. Please do not turn us away your Excellency!

The Archbishop looks at the faces of all the seminarians and gets a look of pity and pain in his face.

> **ARCHBISHOP MARCEL LEFEBVRE**
> I am almost 65 years old. As you know we retire at 65. I just don't think I have the energy to start something new.

> **CLERIC AULAGNIER**
> Your Excellency please excuse my bravado and candidness, but if you do not help us we will be lost and quite honestly have no reason to continue as seminarians in such an environment.

> **ARCHBISHOP MARCEL LEFEBVRE**
> WOW! Who ever advised you to seek me out must have told you of my nature. How can I refuse a good priestly vocation. BUT, since this is very sudden I want you to allow me time to pray on this matter. We should never take on anything without praying first. And I want you all to say a Novena to Our Mother of Perpetual Help. Our Lady will guide our efforts.

(CONTINUED)

MARCEL: The Right Hand of God
CONTINUED:

> **CLERIC COTTARD**
> Thank you your Excellency, we will and look forward to your assistance. Can we have your blessing before we leave?

> **ARCHBISHOP MARCEL LEFEBVRE**
> But of Course!

The Archbishop raises his hands to bless the seminarian and they all drop to their knees.

CUT TO:

INT. - NIGHT - LITHUANIAN HOUSE - ROME - 1969

The Archbishop waits about a week before acting on the request from the seminarians. He is sitting in an office at the Lithuanian House and he decides to pick up the phone and call The Holy Ghost Fathers Swiss province to Bishop Charriere.

> **ARCHBISHOP MARCEL LEFEBVRE**
> Hello you Excellency this is Archbishop Lefebvre.

Bishop Charriere pauses for a few seconds being that he was somewhat caught by surprise being called by the former Superior General of his order. Then responds.

> **BISHOP CHARRIERE**
> Yes, Yes! Your Excellency what a pleasant surprise! How can I help you?

> **ARCHBISHOP MARCEL LEFEBVRE**
> I need you do me a favor. I was approach by quite a few seminarians who are in the French Seminary here in Rome. They have grave concerns over their formation at the Seminary.

> **BISHOP CHARRIERE**
> Okay, how can I help in this matter?

(CONTINUED)

MARCEL: The Right Hand of God
CONTINUED:

>   ARCHBISHOP MARCEL LEFEBVRE
> Can you possibly find a way for
> them to attend the University of
> Fribourg?

>   BISHOP CHARRIERE
> Of course! But do you feel this
> will be a resolution to the issues
> they face at the French Seminary or
> maybe just some of the same?

>   ARCHBISHOP MARCEL LEFEBVRE
> Well your Excellency your concerns
> are well founded but I thought that
> I may be able to monitor the
> situation much better if they were
> in my order.

>   BISHOP CHARRIERE
> My pleasure your Excellency! Does
> it not seem like a life time ago
> that we were in Dakar together? Due
> to what I am seeing lately, I
> thought I would never say it, but
> those were the good old days.

>   ARCHBISHOP MARCEL LEFEBVRE
> Your Excellency my true feelings
> are that we didn't accomplish
> anything compared to what is
> required of us now.

>   BISHOP CHARRIERE
> I am assuming you are referring to
> the Council?

>   ARCHBISHOP MARCEL LEFEBVRE
> Yes, the council if that is what
> they still want to call it.

>   BISHOP CHARRIERE
> Well, I will do all I can to assist
> you in this matter. When will they
> be arriving?

>   ARCHBISHOP MARCEL LEFEBVRE
> Would you mind if I sent several of
> them right away?

(CONTINUED)

MARCEL: The Right Hand of God
CONTINUED:

> BISHOP CHARRIERE
> Of course! I will advise my staff.
> It was great speaking with you and
> I must say I was completely
> depressed over the way you were
> treated by the General Chapter.

> ARCHBISHOP MARCEL LEFEBVRE
> Water under the Bridge your
> Excellency, time to get back to
> work. But thank you for your kind
> words.

FADE OUT.

FADE IN:

INT - DAY - HOLY GHOST FATHERS SWISS PROVINCE

The Archbishop decided to visit the seminarians after a month at the Holy Ghost Seminary in Fribourg. The scene opens with the Archbishop walking up to the front door with his bags in his hands when one of the seminarians comes out to help him.

> CLERIC AULAGNIER
> Hello your Excellency, so very good
> to see you. How was your travels?

> ARCHBISHOP MARCEL LEFEBVRE
> Very good, very good. How are you
> all getting along?

> CLERIC AULAGNIER
> We would like to meet with you to
> discuss if you have the time.

> ARCHBISHOP MARCEL LEFEBVRE
> That's the reason I am here so lets
> sit and discuss.

The Archbishop walks through the halls of the seminary exchanging pleasantries with the priests and teachers along his way as he heads for a meeting room. When they get to the meeting room the Archbishop see's the other seminarians he met before all waiting in the room with very pensive looks on their faces. He closes the door very slowly as if to signal that this will be an unpleasant meeting.

(CONTINUED)

MARCEL: The Right Hand of God
CONTINUED:

>   ARCHBISHOP MARCEL LEFEBVRE (CONT'D)
>   Okay, let me have it! Your looks
>   remind me of the soldiers caring
>   water to the wounded.
>
>   CLERIC COTTARD
>   Your Excellency we want to first
>   thank you for taking the time to
>   speak with the Bishop and getting
>   so personally involved in our
>   formation.
>
>   ARCHBISHOP MARCEL LEFEBVRE
>   But? Come on let me know what is
>   going on.
>
>   CLERIC AULAGNIER
>   Your Excellency, we are not going
>   to remain for long.
>
>   ARCHBISHOP MARCEL LEFEBVRE
>   Why? What is happening?
>
>   CLERIC AULAGNIER
>   We are not receiving any formation.
>   They are not giving us anything.
>
>   CLERIC COTTARD
>   No spiritual conferences, nothing
>   at all.
>
>   CLERIC AULAGNIER
>   With things the way they are, we
>   cannot possible stay.
>
>   ARCHBISHOP MARCEL LEFEBVRE
>   Oh, this is worrisome. Something
>   must be done. Let me have a
>   discussion with Bishop Charriere.
>   Let me see what I can do to get to
>   the bottom of this.

                                                      CUT TO:

INT - DAY - BISHOP CHARRIERE OFFICE - SAME DAY

The Bishops Secretary greets the Archbishop as he is waiting in a side room from the Bishops office.

(CONTINUED)

MARCEL: The Right Hand of God
CONTINUED:

> BISHOP CHARRIERE SECRETARY
> Your Excellency, the Bishop is ready to meet with you. I feel awful for not offering you anything to drink, I will have something brought in. Would you like a sandwich or something to eat?

> ARCHBISHOP MARCEL LEFEBVRE
> No thank you, but a cup of coffee would be nice.

The Secretary nods with approvement and signals the Archbishop to follow him into the Bishops office.

> BISHOP CHARRIERE
> Your Excellency, please excuse my delay. Come in, come in!

> ARCHBISHOP MARCEL LEFEBVRE
> It is so good to see you after all these years. What, almost 20 years?

> BISHOP CHARRIERE
> At least! The last time we were together we were swatting the flies in Dakar.

> ARCHBISHOP MARCEL LEFEBVRE
> Your Excellency, I have met with the seminarians I sent to the Seminary in Fribourg.

> BISHOP CHARRIERE
> Yes! How they getting along? I was meaning to pay a visit myself but my schedule is ridiculous.

> ARCHBISHOP MARCEL LEFEBVRE
> First, I want to thank you for expediting the matter so quickly for me.

> BISHOP CHARRIERE
> Nothing at all. How are they doing?

> ARCHBISHOP MARCEL LEFEBVRE
> Not very good. They claim they are not getting any formation at all, and want to leave.
> (MORE)

MARCEL: The Right Hand of God
CONTINUED:

> ARCHBISHOP MARCEL LEFEBVRE (CONT'D)
> Is there somewhere in Fribourg which would be better than Holy Ghost seminary.

> BISHOP CHARRIERE
> I was afraid that was what your meeting was about. I tried to call ahead of our meeting but know body seemed to know anything. Probably didn't want to know or could care less.

> ARCHBISHOP MARCEL LEFEBVRE
> Can you help me with this matter?

> BISHOP CHARRIERE
> You know, your Excellency, the situation right now is very bad and is getting worse and worse. I am very pessimistic about the future for the diocese itself and the priestly formation.

> ARCHBISHOP MARCEL LEFEBVRE
> How could it have changed that drastically? I only stepped down a year ago and I surely would have notice this while still Superior General.

> BISHOP MARCEL LEFEBVRE
> No. You were shielded from most of this since you had way too much to do.

> ARCHBISHOP MARCEL LEFEBVRE
> Our Holy Father, Pope Pius XII told me this would be the case?

> BISHOP CHARRIERE
> What do you mean?

(CONTINUED)

MARCEL: The Right Hand of God
CONTINUED:

> **ARCHBISHOP MARCEL LEFEBVRE**
> When he elevated me to Archbishop and I questioned him as to why he does not handle certain matters rather quickly, he responded that I too would become so busy and have to delegate so much that I won't possible be able to know what is going on everywhere and I would simply have to trust on those appointed.

> **BISHOP CHARRIERE**
> I understand your Excellency but Pope Pius XII did not have to deal with the shenanigans of Vatican II. It is as if everyone has either lost their faith or their minds.

> **ARCHBISHOP MARCEL LEFEBVRE**
> Maybe not but he predicted it.

> **BISHOP CHARRIERE**
> I am pessimistic; I do not know how things are going to turn out. In any case, yes, we do have an interdiocesan seminary which serves all the Swiss diocese and even accepts secular students. So it could very well receive your students also. I would suggest you inquire there. You still have quite following and they should grant you this small favor.

> **ARCHBISHOP MARCEL LEFEBVRE**
> Your Excellency thank you so much for assisting me in this matter. I will not forget your help.

> **BISHOP CHARRIERE**
> Your Excellency, I thought for sure when you resigned your Superior General position you would just retire. You have done so much for the order and worked so hard. It is now time for you to rest. You earned it.

(CONTINUED)

MARCEL: The Right Hand of God
   CONTINUED:

>   ARCHBISHOP MARCEL LEFEBVRE
>   I thought so too, but I think my
>   work may have just begun. I can't
>   abandon these seminarians or the
>   Church at this time.
>
>   BISHOP CHARRIERE
>   I will pray for you. Good Luck with
>   your seminarians as well.
>
>   ARCHBISHOP MARCEL LEFEBVRE
>   The prayers we will surely need, as
>   for luck I only rely on Divine
>   Providence.
>
>   FADE OUT.

FADE IN:

INT - DAY - INTERDIOCESAN SEMINARY - NEXT DAY

The Archbishop decided to see the interdiocesan seminary before taking the seminarians to yet another problem. The scene opens with the Archbishop knocking at the door of the seminary. The secretary of the Superior greets the Archbishop.

>   INTERDIOCESAN SEMINARY SECRETARY
>   Greetings your Excellency, the
>   Superior is awaiting your arrival.
>
>   ARCHBISHOP MARCEL LEFEBVRE
>   Thank you, is this a good time for
>   him?
>
>   INTERDIOCESAN SEMINARY SECRETARY
>   Of course your Excellency.

The Archbishop follow the secretary down a long hall way to the superior office.

>   SUPERIOR INTERDIOCESAN SEMINARY
>   Your Excellency, our pleasure to
>   receive you. How was your trip?
>
>   ARCHBISHOP MARCEL LEFEBVRE
>   Very good. Is this a good time for
>   you?

                                                    (CONTINUED)

MARCEL: The Right Hand of God
CONTINUED:

>   SUPERIOR INTERDIOCESAN SEMINARY
> Yes, Bishop Charriere informed me
> that you have several seminarians
> that are having some problems with
> their formation. Is that correct?

>   ARCHBISHOP MARCEL LEFEBVRE
> Yes, can you help?

>   SUPERIOR INTERDIOCESAN SEMINARY
> We accept secular students, so we
> are certainly willing to take in a
> few additional seminarians who
> would go to the university. That is
> not a problem.

>   ARCHBISHOP MARCEL LEFEBVRE
> Thank you Superior.

>   SUPERIOR INTERDIOCESAN SEMINARY
> The problem however is, to be
> frank, the seminarians here do not
> receive any special formation.

>   ARCHBISHOP MARCEL LEFEBVRE
> No formation? Why?

>   SUPERIOR INTERDIOCESAN SEMINARY
> They board here, do what they want,
> and organize themselves as they
> wish; but as far as we are
> concerned, they are not our
> responsibility.

>   ARCHBISHOP MARCEL LEFEBVRE
> No formation, not your
> responsibility? Is this a seminary
> or a hotel resort?

The Superior acts dis interested in the Archbishop objection
and simply continues.

>   SUPERIOR INTERDIOCESAN SEMINARY
> If they desire, they may very
> easily have and follow their own
> rule of life; they may very easily
> do their spiritual exercises among
> themselves, together, in the
> chapel. No problem. But don't count
> in us for anything.
>   (MORE)

(CONTINUED)

MARCEL: The Right Hand of God
CONTINUED:

          SUPERIOR INTERDIOCESAN SEMINARY
We will lodge and feed them, but that is the extent of it.

          ARCHBISHOP MARCEL LEFEBVRE
Unbelievable! I remember a time when our Priest were not only formally trained and educated but devoted enough that when they became priests they gave their lives in the missions. Gave their lives for their vocation. These boys.. These priests were only 27 to 29 years old. Now, it is as if the Church has lost its faith and seminarians are being left to their own desires. What kind of formation is this? Where does this come from?

          SUPERIOR INTERDIOCESAN SEMINARY
As you know your Excellency, we are not in the good ole days anymore we are in the new times the new order of things. Time to change with the times.

          ARCHBISHOP MARCEL LEFEBVRE
New times? New Times? You mean heretical times and times of apostasy don't you? This isn't a seminary, no this is a country club.

          SUPERIOR INTERDIOCESAN SEMINARY
I am sorry you feel that way. I assume you do not want you seminarians to join us here.

          ARCHBISHOP MARCEL LEFEBVRE
Never! They will be in the exactly the same position, if not worse, as they were with the Holy Ghost Fathers. Thank you for your time Superior. I will let myself out.

The Archbishop rises slowly as his age is starting to catch up with him. He walks down the hallway very slowly scratching his head and then he begins to talk to himself.

MARCEL: The Right Hand of God
CONTINUED:

>   ARCHBISHOP MARCEL LEFEBVRE (CONT'D)
>   The official liturgy is again going
>   to be the new liturgy, and
>   everything else will also be
>   changed. So what good will it do
>   them to go here? There is no
>   discipline; they can go out
>   anytime, even during the night.
>   That is not acceptable. I cannot be
>   responsible for the formation of
>   seminarians under these conditions.
>   I simply can not! But was is to be
>   done? The Blessed Mother will not
>   abandon them. I just need to think
>   on this further.

FADE OUT.

FADE IN:

INT. - DAY - LITHUSNISN HOUSE - ROME - WEEK LATER

The Archbishop is saying his breviary when a Sister walks in to tell him he has a phone call.

>   SISTER GABRIELLA MARIE
>   Your Excellency, you have a phone
>   call from Fr. Philippe, do wish to
>   take it?
>
>   ARCHBISHOP MARCEL LEFEBVRE
>   Do you know what he is calling
>   about?
>
>   SISTER GABRIELLA MARIE
>   He said he is calling in regards to
>   the seminarians.
>
>   ARCHBISHOP MARCEL LEFEBVRE
>   Okay. Can you just have him hold
>   until I finish my breviary?
>
>   SISTER GABRIELLA MARIE
>   Yes your Excellency.

The Archbishop takes a few minutes to finish his breviary and then picks up the phone.

(CONTINUED)

MARCEL: The Right Hand of God
   CONTINUED:

>   ARCHBISHOP MARCEL LEFEBVRE
>   Hello, this is Archbishop Lefebvre,
>   how can I help you Father?
>
>   FR. PHILIPPE
>   Hello your Excellency, as you know
>   Mr. Bernard Fay, Fr. D'Hauterive
>   and others at the Fribourg
>   University understand you have some
>   problems with a few seminarians. We
>   believe we can help. We must help.
>
>   ARCHBISHOP MARCEL LEFEBVRE
>   Our Blessed Mother never lets me
>   down Father. I was at wits end as
>   what to do for these poor
>   seminarians. What is your thought?
>
>   FR. PHILIPPE
>   Your Excellency can you meet us at
>   Mr. Bernard Fays home. We really
>   need your help as well.
>
>   ARCHBISHOP MARCEL LEFEBVRE
>   Of course. I will come. Just send
>   me the address and I will join you
>   as soon as possible.
>
>   FR. PHILIPPE
>   Thank you your Excellency.

                                                    CUT TO:

THE FRIBOURG GANG

INT - NIGHT - MR. BERNARD FAYS HOME - LATER THAT WEEK

The scene opens with Mr. Bernard Fay, Fr. Philippe, Fr.
D'Hauterive and two other University professors present. They
have cups of coffee around a coffee table as they all huddle
around for a discussion. Fr. Philippe starts the
conversation.

>   FR. PHILIPPE
>   Your Excellency, you have to do
>   something; you cannot just leave
>   these seminarians as they are, like
>   this.

                                                    (CONTINUED)

MARCEL: The Right Hand of God
CONTINUED:

                ARCHBISHOP MARCEL LEFEBVRE
        But I never said ..

Fr. D'Hauterive cuts the Archbishop off

                FR. D'HAUTERIVE
        Excuse me your Excellency, We will
        be sure to send you others; it will
        not be difficult. We already know
        of several who desire to receive a
        real formation. The formation we
        all received.

                MR. BERNARD FAY
        Your Excellency we will do all we
        can to assist with the finances if
        we must.

The Archbishop scans all their faces to make sure they are done before he begins. Then he flashes a huge smile before talking, but it turns to one of concern very quickly. He can tell he is a very tough position and all he can hear is Pope Pius XII's plea to him to stay vigilant and never stop the good fight.

                ARCHBISHOP MARCEL LEFEBVRE
        Thank you for calling me to meet
        with you. You truly are good
        priests and laymen. Your concerns
        are very well founded.

Mr. Fay cuts him off

                MR. BERNARD FAY
        Good then you will help us. You
        will help the seminarians?

                FR. PHILIPPE
        Mr Fay, please let your Excellency
        finish.

                MR. BERNARD FAY
        Excuse me your Excellency.

                ARCHBISHOP MARCEL LEFEBVRE
        No that is quite alright. I share
        your passion. However, I am 65
        years old and I have to start all
        over again.

MARCEL: The Right Hand of God
   CONTINUED:

> FR. D'HAUTERIVE
> But your Excellency we will help you.

> ARCHBISHOP MARCEL LEFEBVRE
> I am sure you will. I am happy to try and help these seminarians. I am willing to find money for them to pay their room and board, and I will be happy to direct them a little in their studies; I am very willing to help them.

> FR. PHILIPPE
> How can we assist?

> ARCHBISHOP MARCEL LEFEBVRE
> We can all help to find them a priest, a chaplain who will take an interest in them, something like that is just fine! But as far as me personally, I am in Rome now and I have no intention of leaving. I am not interested in beginning a new undertaking.

> FR. D'HAUTERIVE
> Your Excellency you don't understand. Without your help we will not have a chance. We can't possibly get the approval or clearance to move forward. We must have you!

> FR. PHILIPPE
> He is so right your Excellency. With a former Superior General of a religious order we will have half a chance to succeed. Please reconsider!

> MR. BERNARD FAY
> We implore your help your Excellency.

The Archbishop has a flashback to Pope Pius XII saying *"Stay Vigilant, stand firm do waiver in the tradition. A time will come when you will need to stand up and take a firm position. Don't waver when called"* Then Fr. Philippe calls out to him as if to wake him from a sleep.

(CONTINUED)

MARCEL: The Right Hand of God
CONTINUED:

>   FR. PHILIPPE
> Your Excellency, can you, will you help us?
>
>   ARCHBISHOP MARCEL LEFEBVRE
> Fine! Listen, it is simple. Since you insist, it will be Bishop Charriere who decides. I am retired and don't have the authority without him. He will decide. I know Bishop Charriere, Bishop of Fribourg. I will go see him. If he encourages me to go ahead, fine, I will see if I can organize something for these seminarians.
>
>   FR. D'HAUTERIVE
> Thank is wonderful your Excellency!
>
>   FR. PHILIPPE
> I knew we could count on your Excellency!
>
>   ARCHBISHOP MARCEL LEFEBVRE
> If Bishop Charriere does not agree, then I will not do anything or will do only what he tells me.
>
>   FR. PHILIPPE
> Agreed.

                                              CUT TO:

INT - DAY - BISHOP CHARRIERE OFFICE - FOLLOWING WEEK

The scene opens with Bishop Charriere serving the Archbishop a cup of tea.

>   BISHOP CHARRIERE
> Your Excellency, how did the Interdiocesean Seminary work for your seminarians?
>
>   ARCHBISHOP MARCEL LEFEBVRE
> Your Excellency, I have not come to talk to you about the interdiocesean seminary but something entirely different.

                                              (CONTINUED)

MARCEL: The Right Hand of God
CONTINUED:

> **BISHOP CHARRIERE**
> Yes please, what is it?

> **ARCHBISHOP MARCEL LEFEBVRE**
> I am considering opening a seminary for these seminarians for proper formation but I need your approval of course and your blessing as well.

> **BISHOP CHARRIERE**
> That is a very easy decision for me. My answer is YES, YES, by all means. The situation is very serious, but you will see that things are getting even worse. So please do it! I beg you to do it.

> **ARCHBISHOP MARCEL LEFEBVRE**
> Your Excellency I never expected you would be so supporting of this.

> **BISHOP CHARRIERE**
> Absolutely! Look for something here in the city; rent a building; put your seminarians there and take care of them; otherwise they will not receive a proper formation. You must do something for them. You must not abandon them.

> **ARCHBISHOP MARCEL LEFEBVRE**
> Okay, since you are the voice of Providence, we will see what we can do. I will think about it and then see if accommodations can be found. You just made Mr. Bernard Fay, fr. Philippe, Fr. D'Hauterive and several other seminary professors very happy.

> **BISHOP CHARRIERE**
> If they are the one's who lead you back to me, I am the one who is grateful. I give you my blessings and gratitude.

FADE OUT.

FADE IN:

MARCEL: The Right Hand of God

THE SALESIAN SOLUTION

The next scenes show various shots of Archbishop Lefebvre and the rest of the group looking for a building. Meeting with owners and pointing out buildings in Fribourg. The scenes end with a close up shot of Marly Street sign and then panning over to the Fathers of Don Bosco talking with the Archbishop and the Fribourg gang.

      SALESIAN FATHER
So your Excellency, you can rent the entire floor of our house. This should enable you to have a chapel and enough bedrooms to lodge 10 seminarians. We can also provide you a separate refectory if you wish.

      ARCHBISHOP MARCEL LEFEBVRE
That would be very good Father. Do you have no need of the facilities?

      SALESIAN FATHER
We lodged students here hoping that some of them would have a Salesian vocation, but unlike in your case your Excellency the vocations for the Salesian order are rare.

      ARCHBISHOP MARCEL LEFEBVRE
That's the new dilemma the Church has Father.

      SALESIAN FATHER
I must say the Blessed Mother must have brought you to us. I am very happy to rent out the unused space and since I am the only one taking care of the facilities it will be nice to have you here. Plus it will help me balance my budget.

      ARCHBISHOP MARCEL LEFEBVRE
Father, I knew when I was looking for a facility that somehow the Salesian's would be the Solution! Thank you so very much.

                  (CONTINUED)

MARCEL: The Right Hand of God
CONTINUED:

> **SALESIAN FATHER**
> Archbishop it is my pleasure and I will do all I can to help in your endeavor. Maybe you will be able to teach me how to get my own vocations up in the mean time.

FADE OUT.

FADE IN:

> **FR. WALTER JAEGER**
> So how long did they say at the Salesian House? Did they get many seminarians right away?

> **FR. MICHAEL GABRIELLI**
> The Salesians were very good to them but they only stayed for a year. But during that period, they simply waited to see who the Blessed Mother would send to them. The Archbishop was a true believer in Divine Providence as you know.

> **FR. WALTER JAEGER**
> So did more seminarians join them?

> **FR. MICHAEL GABRIELLI**
> Yes, Mr. Auglagnier, Mr. Tissier de Mallerais, Mr. Pellabeuf and 6 others who were sent by Fr. Philippe and other friends in Fribourg.

> **FR. WALTER JAEGER**
> The Fribourg Gang hey?

> **FR. MICHAEL GABRIELLI**
> Yes! But at that time the Archbishop was still doing some work for the Congregation of Propaganda and had not yet completely dedicated himself to this work with the seminary. He was acting more as the spokesman and leader.

> **FR. WALTER JAEGER**
> Did they provide full seminary courses at the Salesian House?

(CONTINUED)

MARCEL: The Right Hand of God
CONTINUED:

> FR. MICHAEL GABRIELLI
> No. The seminarians would do their philosophical and theological studies at the University of Fribourg; there would not be, strictly speaking seminary courses given in the Salesian house.

> FR. WALTER JAEGER
> So what purpose did it serve?

> FR. MICHAEL GABRIELLI
> It would simply give a spiritual setting to help them do their studies and be formed spiritually, sacerdotally.

> FR. WALTER JAEGER
> Who ran the house?

> FR. MICHAEL GABRIELLI
> The Archbishop found a priest, Fr. Clerc to run the house and thank god he did.

> FR. WALTER JAEGER
> Why?

> FR. MICHAEL GABRIELLI
> The Archbishop became very ill at that time as was hospitalized for a long time. They couldn't figure out what was causing him to lose so much weight and appetite, he was in unbelievable pain. They finally discovered he has "strongyles" that were eating his liver. But finally he returned.

> FR. WALTER JAEGER
> So did the number of seminarians increase immediately?

> FR. MICHAEL GABRIELLI
> No. At first he actually started to lose seminarians. It was a tough time because the world was changing and society made it almost impossible to keep the vocations.
> (MORE)

(CONTINUED)

MARCEL: The Right Hand of God
CONTINUED:

> **FR. MICHAEL GABRIELLI (CONT'D)**
> But then he received 11 new seminarians and it began to look very promising.

FADE OUT.

FADE IN:

INT - SALESIAN HOUSE - 1970

The scene opens with several seminarians approaching the Archbishop as he walks in the front door of the house.

> **ARCHBISHOP MARCEL LEFEBVRE**
> Hello Boys, how goes the studies?

> **MR. AULAGNIER**
> Your Excellency, what will become of us after the seminary?

> **MR. TISSIER DE MALLERAIS**
> Yes, where are we going?

> **ARCHBISHOP MARCEL LEFEBVRE**
> Well, you will return to your diocese, and you will work in your diocese of course.

> **MR. TISSIER DE MALLERAIS**
> But your Excellency the Bishops will never agree to received us!

> **ARCHBISHOP MARCEL LEFEBVRE**
> What do you mean?

> **MR. TISSIER DE MALLERAIS**
> If we hold fast to the Tradition, if we continue to wear the cassock, if we want to hold on to all that.

> **MR. AULAGNIER**
> They surely will never accept us! No matter where we go, we will be sent away. We will never be able to work in the diocese.

> **MR. TISSIER DE MALLERAIS**
> We will be sheep lead to the slaughter if we go to the diocese.

(CONTINUED)

MARCEL: The Right Hand of God
CONTINUED:

The Archbishop starts to scratch his partially unshaven face and thinks about what they are saying. It as if he never thought it fully through and then all of a sudden is awoken to the real problem for the first time.

> ARCHBISHOP MARCEL LEFEBVRE
> My sweat Jesus! Boys you are right. I above all know what has been going on and haven't thought about that aspect. But what can be done?

> MR. TISSIER DE MALLERAIS
> Can we not stay together your Excellency?

> MR. AULAGNIER
> We must stay together! A society must be founded to unite us together.

> MR. TISSIER DE MALLERAIS
> Yes! Then we must try to find a bishop who will accept us your Excellency. A bishop who will allow us to work together to continue the Tradition. Otherwise all the work you have done so far will simply fall apart.

> ARCHBISHOP MARCEL LEFEBVRE
> You know you might be right. We will try to found a Society. Nevertheless it will need to be approved. So before anything else, lets work on the statutes. I will draw them up and bring them to Bishop Charriere.

> MR. TISSIER DE MALLERAIS
> Will the Bishop support this idea?

> ARCHBISHOP MARCEL LEFEBVRE
> If the Bishop accepts them, good, but it will surprise me. He knows we are traditionalists. He will soon have served his time; he is planning to hand in his resignation in January. He will not want to get involved in something like this. But we will see.
> (MORE)

(CONTINUED)

MARCEL: The Right Hand of God
CONTINUED:

>   ARCHBISHOP MARCEL LEFEBVRE (CONT'D)
>   We will place it in our Blessed
>   Mothers hands as always. She will
>   bring it to our Blessed Lord.
>
>   MR. TISSIER DE MALLERAIS
>   How can she refused your
>   Excellency?
>
>   ARCHBISHOP MARCEL LEFEBVRE
>   Well, lets remember it is always
>   God's will we serve and not ours.
>   Even when we are determined we are
>   on the right track, divine
>   providence always seems to have
>   another path. But we shall see.

                                                    CUT TO:

THE SSPX STATUTES

INT - HOLY GHOST FATHERS SWISS PROVINCE - BISHOP CHARRIERE OFFICE

The scene opens with the Archbishop handing the Bishop with the statutes.

>   ARCHBISHOP MARCEL LEFEBVRE
>   Your Excellency here are the
>   statutes I spoke to you about over
>   the phone.
>
>   BISHOP CHARRIERE
>   Fine, I will study this, please
>   come back after vacation and we
>   will see.
>
>   ARCHBISHOP MARCEL LEFEBVRE
>   Very good your Excellency
>
>   BISHOP CHARRIERE
>   How are the Salesian's treating
>   you?
>
>   ARCHBISHOP MARCEL LEFEBVRE
>   At first they were wonderful to us,
>   they allowed us to get started, but
>   than the priest reported to his
>   provincial.
>   (MORE)

                                                (CONTINUED)

MARCEL: The Right Hand of God
CONTINUED:

ARCHBISHOP MARCEL LEFEBVRE (CONT'D)
He said *"They are traditionalists, they refuse to say the new mass; they always say the old mass. We cannot allow them to stay here with us, it is just impossible"*

BISHOP CHARRIERE
And that it - right? Your out?

ARCHBISHOP MARCEL LEFEBVRE
Yes. They asked us to find a new location. Pushing very hard for us to leave now.

BISHOP CHARRIERE
So at first your helped him balance his budget. But even that has its limits - unbelievable. This absolute hatred for the Latin Mass.

ARCHBISHOP MARCEL LEFEBVRE
Your Excellency you can't blame these poor Priests, they are all being told what to do and the true mass has no room in the Church today.

BISHOP CHARRIERE
What are your plans? Where will you go?

ARCHBISHOP MARCEL LEFEBVRE
As I told the seminarians, our Blessed Mother will help us and divine providence will guide us.

BISHOP CHARRIERE
I will be back to you shortly on your request and as always I will prayer for you your Excellency.

FADE OUT.

FADE IN:

THE ECON SOLUTION

MARCEL: The Right Hand of God

INT - DAY - SALESIAN HOUSE

One of the seminarians walks into the Archbishop's office and informs him he has a call from France.

> MR. TISSIER DE MALLERAIS
> Your Excellency their is a gentlemen calling from France, do you want to take the call.

> ARCHBISHOP MARCEL LEFEBVRE
> Did he say what it was in regards to?

> MR. TISSIER DE MALLERAIS
> No, just that he was requested to contact you by with Bishop Charriere.

The Archbishop practically jumps on the phone in anticipation.

> ARCHBISHOP MARCEL LEFEBVRE
> Hello, this Archbishop Lefebvre, how can I help you.

> FRENCH CALLER
> Your Excellency, I may be able to help you with your need for a seminary. Are you still looking?

> ARCHBISHOP MARCEL LEFEBVRE
> Yes, yes I am.

> FRENCH CALLER
> Go see my lawyer, Mr. Lovey. He has a building in Valais which he might be able to put at your disposition, a building which formerly belonged to the Canons of the great Saint Bernard.

> ARCHBISHOP MARCEL LEFEBVRE
> Wonderful! Where does Mr. Lovey live?

> FRENCH CALLER
> In Fully.

(CONTINUED)

MARCEL: The Right Hand of God
CONTINUED:

>   ARCHBISHOP MARCEL LEFEBVRE
>   Very good - Thank you so much for
>   your assistance.

                                                    CUT TO:

The Archbishop decides to call a Priest, Fr. Bonvin, he knows in Fully. They went to the French Seminary together.

>   FR. BONVIN
>   Hello this is Fr. Bonvin, how can I
>   help you?

>   ARCHBISHOP MARCEL LEFEBVRE
>   Father, this is Archbishop
>   Lefebvre. I don't know if you
>   remember me but we went to the
>   French Seminary together years ago.

>   FR. BONVIN
>   Marcel Lefebvre? I am sorry your
>   Excellency for being so informal.
>   Yes of course I remember you. How
>   can I be of assistance.

>   ARCHBISHOP MARCEL LEFEBVRE
>   Are you familiar with a gentlemen
>   by the name of Lovey?

>   FR. BONVIN
>   Of course I know him. Why?

>   ARCHBISHOP MARCEL LEFEBVRE
>   Well it seems that he has a
>   building which we might be able to
>   let us use for a type of novitiate,
>   a year of spirituality. I would
>   like to know if it is really
>   feasible.

>   FR. BONVIN
>   That is simple enough. We will
>   invite him to lunch and you can
>   talk to him about it and find out.
>   I can accompany you if you like?

>   ARCHBISHOP MARCEL LEFEBVRE
>   That would be wonderful and yes I
>   would greatly appreciate it if you
>   would join us.

MARCEL: The Right Hand of God

EXT. - DAY - FULLY - FRENCH RESTAURANT

The scene open with Fr. Bovin, Archbishop and Mr. Lovey sitting at an outdoor cafe.

                    MR. LOVEY
          How can I help you your Excellency?

                    ARCHBISHOP MARCEL LEFEBVRE
          I understand that you may have a
          building that was previously owned
          by the The Canons of the Great
          Saint Bernard that you may be
          looking to either sell or lease.

                    MR. LOVEY
          Yes, it is true. We have a building
          which needs to be put to use and it
          was the property of the Great St.
          Bernards. They wanted to sell their
          house at Econe which at one time
          was both their agricultural house
          and a novitiate. They use to raise
          their St. Bernard Dogs there as
          well. We did not want that
          building, which for 600 years had
          been a house of the religious.

                    ARCHBISHOP MARCEL LEFEBVRE
          What became of it afterwards?

                    MR. LOVEY
          It became a house used for many
          different things, even a house of
          ill repute. So when we heard they
          wanted to sell it, five of us from
          Valais got together.

                    FR. BONVIN
          Who were the other men?

                    MR. LOVEY
          Mr. Genoud, Mr. Rausis, Mr. Marcel
          Pedroni and his brother Alphonse
          Pedroni. So then we bought it. Do
          you want to see it?

                    FR. BONVIN
          Do you have any other potential
          buyers or occupants?

                                             (CONTINUED)

MARCEL: The Right Hand of God
CONTINUED:

> MR. LOVEY
> Yes, we actually already offered it to the Carmel of Montelimar which was thinking of settling there, but the building did not suit them.

> ARCHBISHOP MARCEL LEFEBVRE
> And now?

> MR. LOVEY
> At the moment it is being used for some handicapped people, but it does not look likely they will be staying either. Anyway, we can find out. Talk to them about it. If it suits you, great. If not, you can look elsewhere.

> ARCHBISHOP MARCEL LEFEBVRE
> Wonderful, lets go see it and speak with those currently occupying it.

FADE OUT.

FADE IN:

> FR. WALTER JAEGER
> So that was how the Econ property was obtained? What happen to the handicapped.

> FR. MICHAEL GABRIELLI
> The handicapped people decided they would not stay and so the Archbishop was able to move in right away.

> FR. WALTER JAEGER
> Did Bishop Charriere approve of the Society statutes?

> FR. MICHAEL GABRIELLI
> Yes. That was the surest sign to the Archbishop that our Lord had much more work for him to complete. It was November 1, 1970 and the Bishop said: "Yes, yes, I approve of it!
> (MORE)

(CONTINUED)

MARCEL: The Right Hand of God
CONTINUED:

> FR. MICHAEL GABRIELLI (CONT'D)
> I am in complete agreement with it." and with that the Bishop had the canonical approbation of the statutes of the "Society of Pius X founded by Archbishop Lefebvre.

> FR. WALTER JAEGER
> And so at 65 years old the Archbishop found an order. WOW, so now his real life's work was about to begin. How strange. This after he already accomplished so much in his life.

> FR. MICHAEL GABRIELLI
> Yes. But here is the real sign of divine providence. 3 months later Bishop Charriere was replaced by Bishop Mamie. Had bishop Mamie been the Bishop he would have refused. Now that is divine Providence.

CUT TO:

THE SSPX ORDER BEGINS

INT - DAY - VIGNETTAZ HOUSE

The next scene will be the Archbishop walking into the house in Vignettaz

> ARCHBISHOP MARCEL LEFEBVRE

Well here they are! The Statutes of the Society of Pius X and they are approved by Bishop Charriere. We are now an official religious order.

> SSPX SEMINARIANS
> *Shouting and Joyful sounds*

> ARCHBISHOP MARCEL LEFEBVRE
> Men, our work has just begun. As Pope Pius XII said to me: "*We must stay vigilant - we must retain the tradition without compromise.*" We will be challenge as you can not believe. The devil will send his emissaries at us from all directions.
> (MORE)

(CONTINUED)

MARCEL: The Right Hand of God
CONTINUED:

> ARCHBISHOP MARCEL LEFEBVRE (CONT'D)
> If we are not up for the good fight our Blessed Mother and our Lord will take this from us just as fast as they gave to us. VIVA CHRISTO REY!!!!!

THE SALLERON INTERVIEW

INT - DAY - ECON - FEBRUARY 13, 1976

The Archbishop has decided to grant an interview with Louis Salleron of La France Catholique-Ecclesia since SSPX was receiving bad press that they were being disobedient to Rome. This is a significant interview because Pope Paul VI is concerned at what will be said and how it will be said. The scene opens with Louis Salleron greeting the Archbishop with all his note pad in hand and kneeing to kiss the Archbishops ring. Louis Salleron then instructs the Archbishop where to sit for the interview. The Archbishop has a confident yet cautious look in his face as Louis is ready to begin the interview.

> LOUIS SALLERON
> Monseigneur, not only in France, but through out the entire world, there is an immense number of Catholics who have placed their trust in you because the Seminary of Econe seems to them the rampart of their faith during what Father Bouyer has described as "the decomposition of Catholicism". However, many today are troubled because the information they read in the newspapers presents you as disobedient to the Pope.

> ARCHBISHOP MARCEL LEFEBVRE
> It seems to me that, on the contrary, my Seminary is the clearest expression of an attitude of obedience to the Pope, successor of Peter and Vicar of Jesus Christ.

> LOUIS SALLERON
> You have however spoken of the "duty to disobey".

(CONTINUED)

MARCEL: The Right Hand of God
CONTINUED:

>   ARCHBISHOP MARCEL LEFEBVRE
>   Undoubtedly. It is a duty to
>   disobey the prescriptions of those
>   who themselves constitute
>   disobedience to the doctrine of the
>   Church. You have a family. If your
>   children receive in the catechism
>   an official teaching, authorized or
>   imposed, which either distorts or
>   is silent with regard to the truths
>   one must believe, your duty is to
>   disobey those who presume to teach
>   this new catechism to your
>   children. In so doing, you obey the
>   church.
>
>   LOUIS SALLERON
>   Cardinal Villot has stated in
>   writing that you refused to accept
>   control by the competent
>   ecclesiastical authorities. Is that
>   true?
>
>   ARCHBISHOP MARCEL LEFEBVRE
>   It is absolutely false! Besides, I
>   have several times had the pleasure
>   of a visit from Mgr. Adam Bishop of
>   Sion and I have explicitly invited
>   Mgr. Mamie, the Bishop of Lausanne,
>   Geneva and Fribourg, who has always
>   refused to come, because he
>   considered my Seminary illegal,
>   although he declared in his letter
>   suppressing it that the Seminary
>   has lost its legal status.
>
>   LOUIS SALLERON
>   Cardinal Villot also says that you
>   are systematically opposed to the
>   Council. Is that true?
>
>   ARCHBISHOP MARCEL LEFEBVRE
>   It is equally false to say that I
>   am systematically opposed to the
>   Second Vatican Council.
>   (MORE)

(CONTINUED)

MARCEL: The Right Hand of God
CONTINUED:

> ARCHBISHOP MARCEL LEFEBVRE (CONT'D)
> BUT, I am convinced that a Liberal spirit was active at the Council and became apparent frequently in conciliar texts, particularly in certain declarations such as that on religious freedom, the one on non-Christian religions and on the Church in the world. That is why it seems to me very legitimate to have considerable reservations concerning these texts.

> LOUIS SALLERON
> In what way?

> ARCHBISHOP MARCEL LEFEBVRE
> Since authorized theological research calls in question veritable dogmas of our faith, I cannot understand why I should be condemned for discussing certain texts of a council which even the Pope himself has recently affirmed to be non-dogmatic. I am accused of infidelity to the Church while none of these theologians engaged in research is condemned. There are truly two weights and two measures.

> LOUIS SALLERON
> However, it is the Pope himself who seems to think that you do not obey the Church.

> ARCHBISHOP MARCEL LEFEBVRE
> Then there has been a misunderstanding. My thoughts and my will in this matter have always been entirely free from any ambiguity. One day I had occasion to write to the Abbe de Nantes: *"I want you to know that if a Bishop breaks with Rome, it will not be me"*.

> LOUIS SALLERON
> Have you had some discussion with the Pope about this question?

(CONTINUED)

MARCEL: The Right Hand of God
CONTINUED:

> ARCHBISHOP MARCEL LEFEBVRE
> No! It is precisely that which I deplore.

> LOUIS SALLERON
> He has not summoned you in order to let you know his mind on this question?

> ARCHBISHOP MARCEL LEFEBVRE
> No! Not only have I not been invited, but I have never been able to obtain an audience with him, and for that reason I have been wondering if my request for an audience had been presented to him.

> LOUIS SALLERON
> Why?

> ARCHBISHOP MARCEL LEFEBVRE
> Recently a Bishop whom I very much esteem has seen the Holy Father in order to tell him of the upset in his diocese caused by all measures taken against me which seems to represent a condemnation of my work. And the Bishop asked the Holy Father to receive me. The Holy Father begged him to discuss this with Cardinal Villot, who told him *"There can be no question of this. The Pope could change his mind and there would be confusion"* So you see there is a screen between the Holy Father and me.

> LOUIS SALLERON
> In his second letter, the Pope told you that he is perfectly well informed concerning you.

> ARCHBISHOP MARCEL LEFEBVRE
> Since I cannot have a audience with him, I have a right to think that he is not "well informed".

(CONTINUED)

MARCEL: The Right Hand of God
CONTINUED:

                    LOUIS SALLERON (CONT'D)
"*to the council, to the post-conciliar reforms and to the orientations to which the Pope himself is committed*"?

                    ARCHBISHOP MARCEL LEFEBVRE
I find a difficulty in the equivocation which borders on falsehood. From the "*Council*" one proceeds to "*post-conciliar reforms*" and from there to the "*orientations to which the Pope himself is committed.*" One no longer knows what precisely is involved. What is to be understood by the "*orientations to which the Pope himself is committed*"?

                    LOUIS SALLERON
I think what you are being asked is to close the Seminary at Econe.

                  ARCHBISHOP MARCEL LEFEBVRE
But why? It is perhaps the only one that corresponds not only to the tradition of the Church but also to the Decree of Vatican II concerning the training of priests. Moreover, I had occasion one day to say so to Cardinal Garrone, who did not deny it.

                    LOUIS SALLERON
If, instead of asking you to make a badly defined act of submission, the Pope were to give you an express order by a new letter, to close the Seminary of Econe, would you close it?

                  ARCHBISHOP MARCEL LEFEBVRE
After a trial carried out in a proper way according to the elementary norms of natural law and ecclesiastical law, yes, I would agree to close my Seminary.
                        (MORE)

MARCEL: The Right Hand of God
CONTINUED:

> ARCHBISHOP MARCEL LEFEBVRE (CONT'D)
> Let me be told in an explicit and concrete manner what I am being reproached with in my activities and in my writings, and let me be given the elementary right to defend myself with the help of an advocate.

> LOUIS SALLERON
> Despite everything, then, you are an optimist?

> ARCHBISHOP MARCEL LEFEBVRE
> It isn't a question of optimism. I don't know what will happen, and sufficient unto the day is the evil thereof. But I have confidence however because, being supported by the millenary tradition of the Church, which can not possibly have been mistaken, I cannot see how, this being so, I can be the subject of condemnation. The ordeal which the Church is undergoing can be ended only by a return to the principles which make her continuous and everlasting.

Louis Salleron closes his note pad and gives the Archbishop a big smile of acceptance. He then tells the Archbishop he will get him a draft before he prints it. The Archbishop smiles in acceptance and starts to walk away.

> LOUIS SALLERON
> Your Excellency, you know our Holy father will have to reply to this interview.

> ARCHBISHOP MARCEL LEFEBVRE
> But of course! I look forward to it.

THE CONSISTORY ALLOCUTION

INT - DAY - ARCHBISHOPS OFFICE IN ECON - JUNE 3, 1976

A SSPX priest knocks on the Archbishops door and slowly walks in after being invited. He has a copy of the Popes Allocution that was published in "*L'Osservatore Romano*"

(CONTINUED)

MARCEL: The Right Hand of God
CONTINUED:

> SSPX PRIEST
> Your Excellency, our Holy Father has responded to your interview with Louis salleron. It is in the L'Osservatore Romano.

> ARCHBISHOP MARCEL LEFEBVRE
> Should I assume it is not pleasant?

> SSPX PRIEST
> Your Excellency, he seems to have taken great insult by your interview. Would you like me to read it to you?

> ARCHBISHOP MARCEL LEFEBVRE
> Please do.

The room starts to fill up with other Priests as the SSPX Priest begins to read.

> SSPX PRIEST
> *"On the one hand there are those who, under the pretext of a greater fidelity to the church and the magisterium, systematically refuse the teachings of the Council itself, its applications and reforms that stem from it, its gradual application by the Apostolic See and the Episcopal Conferences, under Our authority, will by Christ"*.

> ARCHBISHOP MARCEL LEFEBVRE
> I assume he is speaking of me or I should now say us. But you will notice that our Holy Father fails to make a crucial distinction between the teaching of the Council itself and the reforms claiming to interpret that teaching. Reforms which in many cases can not be justified. Go on father.

> SSPX PRIEST
> *"Discredit is cast upon the authority of the Church in the name of a Tradition to which respect is professed only materially and verbally.*
> (MORE)

(CONTINUED)

MARCEL: The Right Hand of God
CONTINUED:

ARCHBISHOP MARCEL LEFEBVRE (CONT'D)
My name is mentioned. Now I am a leader of all Traditional Catholics. I thought I was just the founder/leader of SSPX. There are millions of Traditional Catholics that do not look to me as their leader. They are lead by the Tradition of the very Church they were born into. Now we are a cult and I am its leader. Pope Pius XII warned me about this approach. Go on Father.

SSPX PRIEST
"It is so painful to take not of this; but how can we not see in such an attitude whatever may be these peoples intentions the placing of themselves outside obedience and communion with the Successor of St. Peter and therefore outside the Church?"

ARCHBISHOP MARCEL LEFEBVRE
So it is now possible to deny any and every fundamental dogma of the faith? To disobey any and every disciplinary law of the Church, even the "Conciliar Church"? To be guilty even of sacrilege; and still not be told that communion with the Successor of St. Peter has been broken, but remain true to the traditional faith, and one is considered "outside the Church"?

SSPX PRIEST
"For this, unfortunately, is the logical consequence, when, that is, it is held as preferable to disobey with the pretext of preserving one's faith intact, and of working in one's own way for the preservation of the Catholic Church, while at the same time refusing to give her effective obedience. And this is said openly".

(CONTINUED)

MARCEL: The Right Hand of God
CONTINUED:

ARCHBISHOP MARCEL LEFEBVRE
"*Pretext of preserving the faith?*" Pretext as in hiding our true intentions. So we now lack sincerity. "*Preservation of the Faith in our own way?*" I thought we were attempting to preserve the faith in a form which has a tradition of centuries behind it.

SSPX PRIEST
"*It is even affirmed that the Second vatican Council is not binding*".

ARCHBISHOP MARCEL LEFEBVRE
Binding in what way? The Council was never a General Council with the authority of the Church's Extraordinary Magisterium under pain of anathema. Even the Pope himself has stated on a number of occasions, the documents of the Council come to us with Authority of the Ordinary Magisterium of the Church. So if they do, they do not carry the same authority.

SSPX PRIEST
"*That the faith would also be in danger because of the reforms and post-conciliar directives; that one had the duty to disobey in order to preserve certain traditions*"

ARCHBISHOP MARCEL LEFEBVRE
But of course! Any faithful Catholic who understands the nature of the post-conciliar directives and the manner in which they are been implemented must repudiate them to preserve the faith and show they take the faith seriously.

(CONTINUED)

MARCEL: The Right Hand of God
CONTINUED:

> SSPX PRIEST
> "What traditions? Is it for this group, not the Pope, not the College of Bishops, not the Ecumenical Council, to decide which among the innumerable tradition must be considered as the norm of faith!"

> ARCHBISHOP MARCEL LEFEBVRE
> The sad truth is that it is clear in practice that neither our Holy Father nor the Bishops are prepared to take practical steps to uphold the basic forms of faith, apart from issuing pious exhortations which they made no effort to implement.

> SPPX PRIEST
> "As you see, Venerable Brethren, such an attitude sets itself up as judge of that divine will which placed Peter and his lawful Successors at the head of the Church to confirm the brethren in the faith, and to feed the universal flock, and which established him as the guarantor and custodian of the deposit of faith"

> ARCHBISHOP MARCEL LEFEBVRE
> This above all is the furthest from the true. I have always upheld papal authority my entire priestly life. I do not challenge Papal Authority. What I have done is question certain specific acts of the Pope and equally important, the failure of our Holy Father to act in defense of the Faith. In doing this I am acting in accordance with approved theological principles.

(CONTINUED)

MARCEL: The Right Hand of God
CONTINUED:

> SPPX PRIEST
> "And this is all the more serious in particular, when division is introduced precisely where congregavit nos in unum Christi amor, in the Liturgy and the Eucharistic Sacrifice, by the refusing of obedience to the norms laid down in the liturgical sphere.

> ARCHBISHOP MARCEL LEFEBVRE
> This is our Holy Fathers most astonishing statement in this allocution. It is the very fact that the post-conciliar liturgical reform which has totally destroyed the unity of the Roman rite. We have not been presented with a new form of Mass, but with an ongoing liturgical revolution, in which anything is tolerated BUT THE TRADITIONAL MASS!

> SPPX PRIEST
> Your Excellency, so in the face of this liturgical anarchy, traditionalists wish to adhere to a form of Mass which in all essentials dates back more than a millennium, for which we are accused of promoting liturgical disunity?

> ARCHBISHOP MARCEL LEFEBVRE
> Exactly. Does this sound like something that would come from a Pope? I suspect it is not. It can not be.

> SSPX PRIEST
> I will continue. "It is in the name of Tradition that we ask all our sons and daughters, all the Catholic communities, to celebrate with dignity and fervor the renewed liturgy".

(CONTINUED)

MARCEL: The Right Hand of God
CONTINUED:

> ARCHBISHOP MARCEL LEFEBVRE
> Our Holy Father must have realized that the liturgy in its present form is a source of misery and even revulsion to countless thousands of the faithful, and that even where they accept it as an act of obedience to expect them to do so with fervor is to ask the impossible.

> SSPX PRIEST
> *"The adoption of the new Ordo Missae is certainly not left to the free choice of priests or faithful. The Instruction of 14 June 1971 has provided with the authorization of the Ordinary, for the celebration of the Mass in the old form only by aged and infirm priests, who offer the divine Sacrifice sine populo."*

> ARCHBISHOP MARCEL LEFEBVRE
> This is a curious statement.

> SPPX PRIEST
> Why your Excellency.

> ARCHBISHOP MARCEL LEFEBVRE
> That our Holy Father makes no reference at all to his Apostolic Constitution Missale Romanum of April 3, 1969 which authorized the introduction of the New Mass.

> SSPX PRIEST
> Why is that significant?

> ARCHBISHOP MARCEL LEFEBVRE
> Because if the Traditional Mass had been prohibited that would have been the only document which could have done so. But it does not. So why would our Holy Father make the statement *"The adoption of the new Ordo Missae is certainly not left to the free choice of priests or faithful"* This is Highly unusual because our Holy Father in essence just prohibited the Traditional Mass. But he can not.

(CONTINUED)

MARCEL: The Right Hand of God
CONTINUED:

                    SSPX PRIEST
So what are you saying? That our Holy Father could not have written this Allocution?

              ARCHBISHOP MARCEL LEFEBVRE
I don't know. I just can't imagine he would dare say that the Mass of over 1,000 years is now prohibited.

                    SSPX PRIEST
Well then his next statement will eliminate any doubt of that. He goes on to say; *"The new ordo was promulgated to take the place of the old, after mature deliberation, following upon the requests of the Second Vatican Council.*

With that statement the Archbishop sits up and then stands up as if he can't believe his ears. He starts to walk around the room looking up and then down and then around as if he is trying to remember when during the council this discussion or conclusion was made.

            ARCHBISHOP MARCEL LEFEBVRE (CONT'D)
It can't be! How can it be? At no time did the Fathers of Vatican II ever authorize the composition of a new order of mass as he says *"to take the place of the old"* They did no more than authorize minor modifications to the existing Mass. I don't believe he is allowed to change the Mass due the Council of Trent.

                    SSPX PRIEST
Our Holy Father must have known that's what you would say. He goes on to say: *"In no different way did Our Holy Predecessor Pius V make obligatory the Missal reformed under his authority, following the Council of Trent"*

              ARCHBISHOP MARCEL LEFEBVRE
This translation of Our Holy Fathers words must be in error. I can not believe he would say such a thing.
                    (MORE)

(CONTINUED)

MARCEL: The Right Hand of God
CONTINUED:

> ARCHBISHOP MARCEL LEFEBVRE (CONT'D)
> It is impossible for him to say "*in no way different way than what Pope Pius V did as obligatory*" Please re-read that for me. Maybe I misunderstand.

The Priest repeats it as originally stated.

> ARCHBISHOP MARCEL LEFEBVRE (CONT'D)
> We must seek out the Pope to confirm this is what he truly meant to say. If it is his own words, he is saying that if something is untrue the fact that it is stated to be true by the Pope cannot alter the fact it is untrue. I never thought I would live to see the day when the Council of Trent was turned on its ear as just a Pope's wishes and not doctrinal. We are now entering a time of complete destruction to the Holy Roman Catholic Church. How can you continue to argue when all the Church has known and supported for over a 1,000 years is determined to be just a whim of a Pope.

> SSPX PRIEST
> Shall I go on?

> ARCHBISHOP MARCEL LEFEBVRE
> Yes please do, although I can only imagine what is left to say after that.

> SSPX PRIEST
> "*With the same supreme authority that comes from Christ Jesus, we call for the same obedience to all the other liturgical, disciplinary and pastoral reforms which have matured in these years in the implementation of the Council decrees. Any initiative which tries to obstruct them cannot claim the prerogative of rendering a service to the Church: in fact it causes the Church serious damage*"

(CONTINUED)

MARCEL: The Right Hand of God
CONTINUED:

> ARCHBISHOP MARCEL LEFEBVRE
> One again, anyone with experience of this new liturgy in practice will know that a faithful Catholic who loves the Mass and loves the Church has no alternative but to try to obstruct this reform which, with all due respect to our Holy Father, DOES NOT proceed from mature deliberation.

> SSPX PRIEST 2
> Your Excellency, with all due respect to our Holy Father as you say. As Christ's Vicar on earth is it not his duty to safeguard the Blessed Sacrament from the sacrilege to which this practice inevitably leads?

> ARCHBISHOP MARCEL LEFEBVRE
> But of course it does! However, he is failing to do so and not for the first time in the history of the Church, the faithful found that their Catholic duty was NOT to follow the example of the Pope.

> SSPX PRIEST 2
> But then we will be considered schismatic, won't we?

> ARCHBISHOP MARCEL LEFEBVRE
> You can not be schismatic if you uphold the doctrinal teaching of the Church. We are not Martin Luther, we are not saying that we will not follow the Church teachings. We are saying we question our Pope and that his rulings and determinations are in error.

(CONTINUED)

CONTINUED:

> SSPX PRIEST
> He goes on to say: "*Various times, directly and through our collaborators and other friendly persons, We have called the attention of Archbishop Lefebrve to the seriousness of his behavior, the irregularity of his principal present initiatives, the inconsistency and often falsity of the doctrinal positions on which he bases this behavior and these initiatives, and the damage that accrues to the entire Church because of them.*"

> ARCHBISHOP MARCEL LEFEBVRE
> If such admonitions have been made they have not been made public. The first admonition of a genuinely doctrinal nature given by the Pope to me was that I should accept the totally false proposition that Vatican II has as much authority as Nicea, and more importance in some respects.

> SSPX PRIEST
> "*It is with profound sadness but with paternal hope that we once more turn to this confrere of Ours, to his collaborators and to those who have let themselves be carried away by them.*

> ARCHBISHOP MARCEL LEFEBVRE
> Who is carrying who away. Less than 10 years ago how were Catholics practicing? Am I carrying any Catholic away or is the Council attempting to carry them away?

(CONTINUED)

MARCEL: The Right Hand of God
CONTINUED:

> SSPX PRIEST
> *"Oh certainly, we believe that many of these faithful at least in the beginning were in good faith: We also understand their sentimental attachment to forms of worship or of discipline that for a long time had been for them a spiritual support and in which they had found spiritual sustenance."*

> ARCHBISHOP MARCEL LEFEBVRE
> So now we are reducing our faith to sentimental attachment. Not spiritual doctrine, not the tradition of our Church? Oh no, we are fighters of the new fad. Go along to get along?

> SSPX PRIEST
> *"But we are confident that they will reflect with serenity, without closed minds, and they will admit that they can find today the support and sustenance that they are seeking in the renewed forms that the Second Vatican Ecumenical Council and we ourself have decreed as being necessary for the good of the Church, her progress in the modern world and her unity."*

> ARCHBISHOP MARCEL LEFEBVRE
> First, does this imply that traditionalists are no longer in good faith? Second, while traditionalists naturally look to the traditional liturgy and devotional practices with a nostalgia which is both right and fitting, their opposition to the "Conciliar Church" and to the liturgical reform in general is based not upon sentiment but on a determination to uphold the faith which these reforms compromise.

> SSPX PRIEST 2
> In what way do you mean your Excellency *"determination to uphold the Faith"*?

(CONTINUED)

MARCEL: The Right Hand of God
CONTINUED:

                      ARCHBISHOP MARCEL LEFEBVRE
It is like this. Examine the prayers which Cranmer removed from the Traditional Mass, as he wrote in "Cranmer's Godly Order". Then compare them to the prayers removed from the Mass under the authority of Pope Paul VI. By what possible stretch of the imagination can it be claimed that it was absolutely essential to remove these prayers, *"For the Good of the Church"*?, *"For the Churches Progress in the World"*? and for the *"Churches Unity*? as he says.

                      SSPX PRIEST
Our Holy father says more *"We therefore exhort yet once again all these brethren and sons and daughters of ours; we beseech them to become aware of the profound wounds that they otherwise cause to the Church, and we invite them again to reflect on Christ's serious warning about unity of the Church and on the obedience that is due to the lawful Pastor placed by him over the universal flock, as a sign of the obedience due to the Father and the Son"*.

                      ARCHBISHOP MARCEL LEFEBVRE
On the contrary, the wounds in the Church and the damage to her unity have not been caused by the stand made by Us and other traditionalists. The Traditionalists have taken their stand as a reaction to these wounds and this disunity. Was it not our Holy Father who stated *"The smoke of Hell has entered the Vatican?"*

                      SSPX PRIEST
"Then may they know how to rediscover in humility and edification the joy of the whole people of God, the way of unity and of love"

MARCEL: The Right Hand of God
CONTINUED:

>   ARCHBISHOP MARCEL LEFEBVRE
> In other words, traditionalists
> will only become acceptable if they
> abandon all that they most love and
> revere and believe to be essential
> to the well-being of the Church and
> accept the entire post-concillar
> revolution without reservation. The
> price is unacceptable. Why not ask
> all Catholics to become Lutherans?
> Or Baptists or Hinduists? If you
> tear the very fabric of the Church
> Doctrine to shreds in hope of
> becoming one with modern times, why
> not just terminate the Church all
> together? We are no longer a
> beacon, no we are just one of many.

>   SSPX PRIEST
> Your Excellency this next statement
> by our Holy Father will have you
> leaping from the window. *"Such
> Christians are not very numerous,
> it is true, but they make much
> noise, believing too easily that
> they are in a position to interpret
> the needs of the entire Christian
> people or the irreversible
> direction of history"*

>   ARCHBISHOP MARCEL LEFEBVRE
> *"needs of the entire Christian
> People"* When has the Church ever
> recognized anyone as being
> Christian that wasn't Catholic. All
> others were always considered
> heretics. But now since the Second
> vatican Council sought to include
> heretical Christians they are
> including them as decision makers.

>   SSPX PRIEST 2
> Why does he refer to
> Traditionalists as *"not very
> numerous"* was not our Church one
> Church in the Tradition prior to
> Vatican II?

(CONTINUED)

MARCEL: The Right Hand of God
CONTINUED:

      ARCHBISHOP MARCEL LEFEBVRE
But of course. However, you will see now that virtually every position of importance in the entire Catholic establishment throughout the West is in the hands of these Liberals; they control all the official commissions, catechetical, liturgical, and ecumenical; all too frequently Episcopal Conferences serve only to act as their mouthpieces, and yet our Holy Father himself claimed that they are few in number and make much noise.

      SSPX PRIEST
That's it your Excellency. If that is not enough.

      ARCHBISHOP MARCEL LEFEBVRE
Fathers, as you know I may be old and many may say as they have said of all my peers who fight for traditionalism, "*The old just fear change!*" But, I tell you there will come a time when the young will stand up and fight and they will say that they are just trouble makers. This is the way of liberals. Our beloved Holy Father Pope Pius XII warned me about this. But most importantly we can never become bitter because the devils influences always seek to increase bitterness. Instead we must pray for this Pope and we must pray for the Holy Catholic Church because truly the "smoke of Hell has entered".

The Archbishop rises to leave the room and walks very slowly down the hall as if he for the first time realizes exactly what his new order and the Catholic Church are in for.

INT. - DAY - ECON - JUNE, 1976

The Archbishops brother Rene comes to visit the Archbishop and is let into his office.

          (CONTINUED)

MARCEL: The Right Hand of God
CONTINUED:

> **FR. RENE LEFEBVRE**
> Marcel! How is my younger defiant brother doing?

> **ARCHBISHOP MARCEL LEFEBVRE**
> Rene it is wonderful to see you, but as I know you better than I know myself, I know this visit must be painful for you.

> **FR. RENE LEFEBVRE**
> Never painful to see you. BUT, Marcel I understand your determination to stand your ground for the proper formation of Priests. I understand your ground to continue with your Traditional ways. BUT, to refuse the Pope is a whole different issue.

> **ARCHBISHOP MARCEL LEFEBVRE**
> Rene what should I do? Should I just let this new Church destroy everything I, We have come to support our entire lives?

> **FR. RENE LEFEBVRE**
> But it is the Pope and the Council you fight. How can you be disobedient to the Holy Father? I understand he warned you not to ordain anymore priests in the tradition and to support the Second Vatican Council. How can you disobey?

> **ARCHBISHOP MARCEL LEFEBVRE**
> It is true. I have been put on notice by the Pope through Mgr Benelli and I responded directly to the Pope as to why I will continue but seek an audience with him. But I simply get another letter from Mgr Benelli telling me that my ordinations will no longer be binding and in essence my order no longer an order.

(CONTINUED)

MARCEL: The Right Hand of God
CONTINUED:

> FR. RENE LEFEBVRE
> So there you have it! Your done! Now simply retire as you should have already and put all this nonsense to an end.

> ARCHBISHOP MARCEL LEFEBVRE
> Nonsense? Do you think this is nonsense? Have you seen the abuses that have gone on under the name of this Second Vatican Council? More than ever I will not stop. More than ever I will take the words of Pope Pius XII with even more conviction *"Never stop, take the stand for Tradition"*.

> FR. RENE LEFEBVRE
> So you will continue with the ordinations this month?

> ARCHBISHOP MARCEL LEFEBVRE
> The ordinations of June 29th will continue as planned. These priests have studied and become legitimate priests the same way you and I have become priests.

> FR. RENE LEFEBVRE
> So there is nothing I can do to save my brother from being thrown out of the Catholic Church?

> ARCHBISHOP MARCEL LEFEBVRE
> If I am in fact thrown out or my priests are expelled, we are doing so under the cause of protecting Holy Mother Church and will never lay down because the pressure is to great. Even if they do send my Brother to me.

> FR. RENE LEFEBVRE
> They didn't send me! They know us Lefebvre's will never betray each other. I just fear for you my Brother. I fear for your soul!

> ARCHBISHOP MARCEL LEFEBVRE
> Fear not! As Pope Pius XII reminded me when I asked *"how will I know"*.
> (MORE)

(CONTINUED)

MARCEL: The Right Hand of God
CONTINUED:

>   ARCHBISHOP MARCEL LEFEBVRE (CONT'D)
> He replied "*By your fruits you
> shall know them*" Rene, their fruits
> are not good. Their fruits are of
> pure modernism, liberalism and
> humanism. Their fruits are not of
> God.
>
>   FR. RENE LEFEBVRE
> But Marcel, Cardinal Villot already
> stated that SSPX ceases to exist
> last October and even warned the
> other bishops not to be involved in
> this upcoming ordination.
>
>   ARCHBISHOP MARCEL LEFEBVRE
> But of course! That's how these
> liberals work. Have you learned
> nothing from our past, from our
> Father's warning, from the German
> Nazi's and the Stalin's of this
> world. Threaten at the same time
> tell everyone they are open to
> dialogue. They dialogue under the
> banner of ecumenicialism, but when
> it comes to the tradition they
> threaten and punish. "*By our fruits
> they shall no us! By their Fruits
> we shall no them!*"

                                        FADE OUT.

FADE IN:

THE ORDINATIONS OF 1976

EXT - DAY - ECON - ORDINATIONS - JUNE 29, 1976

The scene opens with the Archbishop ready to deliver the sermon at the ordination of 13 priests and 13 sub-deacons on the Feast of St. Peter and Paul.

>   ARCHBISHOP MARCEL LEFEBVRE
> In the name of the Father, and the
> Son, and of the Holy Ghost.
>
>   ORDINATION CONGREGATION
> AMEN!

(CONTINUED)

MARCEL: The Right Hand of God
CONTINUED:

>ARCHBISHOP MARCEL LEFEBVRE
>My dear friends, dear confreres, dear brethren who have come from every country, from all horizons: It is a joy for us to welcome you and to feel you so close to us at this moment so important for our Fraternity and also for the Church. I think that, if the pilgrims have permitted themselves to make this sacrifice, to journey day and night, to come from distant regions to participate in this ceremony, it is because they had the conviction that they were coming to participate in a ceremony of the Church, to participate in a ceremony which would fill their hearts with joy, because they now have the certitude in returning to their homes that the Catholic Church continues.

The next scenes should show the Archbishop continuing with his sermon as the camera scans the crowd and then focuses on many of the faces in the crowd. Then the camera focuses on a car in the very back of the ceremony with a up close shot of Cardinal sitting in the back seat with his window down with a priest sitting next to him.

>CARDINAL IN THE CAR
>There you have it. That is the straw that has broken our Holy Fathers back. He has continued with the ordinations in complete disobedience. He has dug his own grave. It is out of our hands now. Even now he speaks if the Roman Curia with such destain.

>PRIEST IN CAR
>You have to give him credit. He is definitely a zealot.

The Cardinal gives the priest a defiant look and the scene comes back to the Archbishop.

>ARCHBISHOP MARCEL LEFEBVRE
>Are we wrong in obstinately wanting to keep the rite of all time?
>(MORE)

(CONTINUED)

MARCEL: The Right Hand of God
CONTINUED:

> ARCHBISHOP MARCEL LEFEBVRE (CONT'D)
> We have, of course, prayed, we have consulted, we have reflected, we have mediated to discover if it is not indeed we who are in error, or if we do not really have a sufficient reason not to submit ourselves to the new rite. And in fact, the very insistence of those who were sent from Rome to ask us to change rite makes us wonder.

> CARDINAL IN THE CAR
> Wonder? Who gave him the right to wonder anything?

> ARCHBISHOP MARCEL LEFEBVRE
> And we have the precise conviction that this new rite of Mass expresses a new faith, a faith which is not ours, a faith which is not the Catholic Faith. This New Mass is a symbol, is an expression, is an image of a new faith, of a Modernist faith. For if the most holy Church has wished to guard throughout the centuries this precious treasure which She has given us of the rite of Holy Mass which was canonized by St. Pope Pius V, it has not been without purpose. It is because this Mass contains Our Whole Faith, the whole Catholic Faith; faith in the Most Holy Trinity, faith in the Divinity of Our Lord Jesus Christ, faith in the Redemption of Our Lord.

The scene moves back to the Cardinal in the car observing.

> CARDINAL IN THE CAR
> So he knows what's best for the Church. He knows better than the Pope himself. Maybe we should just close down the Vatican and all move to Econe and sit at the feet of Archbishop Lefebvre and his new apostles.

MARCEL: The Right Hand of God
CONTINUED:

> PRIEST IN CAR
> I am not getting that out of him your Eminence. He sounds as if he is just sticking to the tradition.

> CARDINAL IN THE CAR
> Tradition? Tradition is dead! Latin is dead! The church moves on and we won't get caught up in the past as the world moves on. If it were up to Archbishop Lefebvre men on the moon would be considered a liberal gesture.

The scene moves back to the Archbishop.

> ARCHBISHOP MARCEL LEFEBVRE
> Now it is evident that the new rite, if I may say so, supposes another conception of the Catholic religion, another religion! It is no longer the priest who offers the Holy Sacrifice of the Mass, it is the assembly. Now this is an entire program. Henceforth it is the assembly also that replaces authority in the Church. It is the assembly of bishops that replaces the power of individual bishops. It is the priests council that replaces the power of the bishop in the diocese. It is numbers that command from now on in the Holy Church. And this is expressed in the Mass precisely because the assembly replaces the priest, to such a point that now many priests no longer want to say the Holy Mass when there is no assembly. Slowly but surely the Protestant notion of the Mass is being introduced into the Holy Church. This is consistent with the mentality of modern man absolutely consistent. For it is the democratic ideal which is the fundamental idea of modern man, that is to say, that the power lies with the assembly, that authority is in the people, in the masses, and not in God.

(CONTINUED)

MARCEL: The Right Hand of God
CONTINUED:

The scene shifts back to the Priest in the Car.

> PRIEST IN CAR
> Your Eminence, this is how it seems things are going in many of the parishes. The parish councils want to run the parish instead of the Pastor.

> CARDINAL IN THE CAR
> Are you now taken in by Lefebrve? Are you kidding? What are you talking about?

> PRIEST IN CAR
> Your Eminence I understand I was to come with you as a witness and I am simply giving my opinion on his sermon. Much of what I am seeing going on in the parishes is very concerning.

> CARDINAL IN THE CAR
> Are you saying I am not in touch with the parishes, that I do not know what is going on in the Church? Is that what you are saying?

> PRIEST IN CAR
> No that is now what I am saying your Eminence. But with all due respect, it seems to me the Parishioners are dictating to the Church. It seems what ever they want they get.

> CARDINAL IN THE CAR
> Like what? In what way?

> PRIEST IN CAR
> If they want to have a guitar mass they demand it. If they want to start holding hands during prayers, they demand it. If they want to talk in the Church they demand it. They simply demand it and it is given to them. Much like the Archbishop is saying, it is the democratic ideal.
> (MORE)

(CONTINUED)

MARCEL: The Right Hand of God
CONTINUED:

> PRIEST IN CAR (CONT'D)
> The masses will tell the Church what to do and they are doing just that.

> CARDINAL IN THE CAR
> This is not the spirit of Vatican II, this is just a poor job on the part of the Pastor or the Bishops.

The scene moves back to the Archbishop.

> ARCHBISHOP MARCEL LEFEBVRE
> And this is what is at present corrupting the entire Church. For by this idea of power bestowed on the lower rank, in the Holy Mass, they have destroyed the Priesthood! They are destroying the priesthood, for what is the priest, if the priest no longer has a personal power, that power which is given to him by his ordination, as these future priests are going to receive it in a moment? They will no longer be men like other men! They will be men of God! They will be men, I should say, who almost participate in the divinity of Our Lord Jesus Christ.

The scene moves to all the priest about to be ordained and then moves across the crowd gathered and then moves to the Cardinal in the car.

> CARDINAL IN THE CAR
> No! It will be men who will not be allowed to practice as Catholic Priests. It will be about men who will move towards excommunication. It will not be about men of Christ!

> PRIEST IN CAR
> So is this why I am here? I am here to be a witness to the expelling of newly ordained Priests? The very same type of ordination I went through to become a priest 25 years ago? Men that went through the same formation as I did? Men that deserve to be priests?

(CONTINUED)

MARCEL: The Right Hand of God
CONTINUED:

> CARDINAL IN THE CAR
> They were warned! They were given ample time to leave the Archbishop!

> PRIEST IN CAR
> Why would they? Why should they? Should we have left our superiors when we were just about to be ordained? Would we have given up 4 years of formation and just left?

> CARDINAL IN THE CAR
> Are you now siding with the Archbishop?

> PRIEST IN CAR
> I am siding with God! If you want me here to witness this ordination than so be it. If you want me here to railroad Archbishop Lefebrve and assist in the expelling of good Priests who deserve to become priests, I will not and I should not your Eminence. Maybe it is best that I take my leave.

> CARDINAL IN THE CAR
> Maybe so!

The Priest in the Car leaves the car and walks among the congregation to take a seat and listen to the Archbishop.

> ARCHBISHOP MARCEL LEFEBVRE
> Let us ask St. Peter and St. Paul to maintain in us this faith in Peter. Ah, yes, we believe in peter, we believe in the Successor of Peter! But as Pope Pius IX says well in his dogmatic constitution, the Pope has received the Holy Ghost, not to make new truths, but to maintain us in the Faith of all time.

The scene switches back to the cardinal in the car speaking to his driver.

> CARDINAL IN THE CAR
> Pope Pius IX, Pope Pius X, Pope Pius XII.
> (MORE)

(CONTINUED)

MARCEL: The Right Hand of God
CONTINUED:

> **CARDINAL IN THE CAR (CONT'D)**
> That is all he quotes are Pope Pius's – Does he have no other formation?

> **DRIVER**
> I'm sorry your Eminence but they were some of our greatest Popes.

> **CARDINAL IN THE CAR**
> BAH! Too Traditional for my blood.

The scene switches back to the Archbishop.

> **ARCHBISHOP MARCEL LEFEBVRE**
> This is the definition of the Pope made at the time of the time of the First Vatican Council by Pope Pius IX. And that is why we are persuaded that, in maintaining these traditions, we are manifesting our love, our docility, our obedience to the Successor of Peter. In the name of the Father and of the Son and of the Holy Ghost.

> **CONGREGATION**
> Amen!

The scene moves back to the cardinal in the car.

> **CARDINAL IN THE CAR**
> Amen is right! I thought he would never finish. He has picked a fine feast day to be disobedient to the Holy Father. This ordination has not affect.

> **DRIVER**
> Are you ready to leave your Eminence?

> **CARDINAL IN THE CAR**
> Yes, I have seen and witnessed enough. Lets go.

FADE OUT.

FADE IN:

MARCEL: The Right Hand of God

THE SUSPENSION

INT - DAY - PRESS BUREAU OF THE HOLY SEE - JULY 1, 1976

Father Romeo Panciroli, spokesman for the Press Bureau of the Holy See is about to make a statement to the press regarding the Suspension of SSPX Priests. There are many reporters in the room and Cardinal Villot is standing somewhat to the side as an observer.

> FR. ROMEO PANCIROLI
> According to information from Switzerland, Mgr. Lefebvre has actually gone ahead with the ordination of a certain number of priests and deacons. Accordingly to the same information, the candidates were not provided with dimissorial letters from their Ordinary or with a valid canonical title. In that case, the following rules of the Code of Canon Law apply:
> 10. Mgr. Lefebvre has automatically incurred suspension for a year from the conferring of orders, a suspension reserved to the Apostolic See. The same is true of earlier ordinations which may have taken place under the same conditions, with the aggravating circumstances, in this case, of irregularity linked with repetition of the offense. This suspension is in addition to the prohibition of conferring pronounced by the Holy Father and transgressed by Mgr. Lefebvre, but which obviously is still valid and operative.
> 20. Those who have been ordained are ipso facto suspended from the order received, and, if they were to exercise it, they would be in an irregular and criminal situation.
> (MORE)

(CONTINUED)

MARCEL: The Right Hand of God

CONTINUED:

> FR. ROMEO PANCIROLI (CONT'D)
> The priests who may have already been suspended for a preceding irregular promotion to the diaconate could be punished with severe penalties according to the circumstance, in addition to the fact that they have put themselves in an irregular situation.
> 30. The Holy See is examining the special case of the formal disobedience of Mgr. Lefebvre to the instructions of the Holy Father who, by the documents of 12 and 25 June 1976, expressly forbade him to proceed with the ordinations. Even fraternal intervention these last days, started by the Holy Father to get Mgr. Lefebvre to abandon his project, could not prevent the interdiction being violated.

FADE OUT.

FADE IN:

It is from here on that Fr. Gabrielli will tell of all the successes and battles SSPX fought up to the time of the Consecration of the Bishops. The scene sequences will be as follows:

> FR. WALTER JAEGER
> So Father what did or could the Archbishop do. The Pope basically shut down his seminary and made all his ordinations null and void.

> FR. MICHAEL GABRIELLI
> Father this is were the real Men of our Church appear. They appear when the times are at their worse. They just know what they are doing is right. They gain a gift from the Holy Spirit that makes then stand tall and continue. If St Thomas Moore was the "Man of all Seasons" then the Archbishop was "The Man of all Centuries - the Right Hand of God" And that is exactly what the Archbishop did, He stood up and picked up his cross and continued.

(CONTINUED)

MARCEL: The Right Hand of God
CONTINUED:

Pictures of the successes of SSPX appear on the screen as follow:

Assembly of the faithful: the summer of 1976 after the Popes condemnation, 10,000 faithful Catholics in Lille come out to show their support of the Archbishop.

February, 1977: Traditional Catholics liberate the Church of St. Nicolas du Chardonnet in Paris. The once dying Church is filled with crowds supporting the Traditional Faith.

September, 1977: 38 new seminarians are admitted, despite condemnations.

October, 1977: SSPX has 40 Priests, 150 Seminarians, 20 Priories, and 3 seminaries. The sisters of the Society, which was founded in 1974, move their novitiate to Albano, and their general house to St. Michel-en-Brenne under the direction of Mother Mary Gabriel Lefebvre.

The 1978 Acquisitions: 4 Priories in France, a property in Long Island, and the priory in Madrid. The Jesuit College of St. Mary's Kansas, is also bought by the Society. The Society opens a seminary in Argentina with 12 candidates.

1978 Pope John Paul II meets with Archbishop: Pope John Paul II receives the Archbishop and after a long conversation the Pope is willing to remove all restrictions on the traditional Mass.

The 1979 Acquisitions: Inn is purchased at Rickenbach (Switzerland) to be the General House for the Society. A large property is bought north of Turin at Montalenghe (Italy), for a retreat house. The American Seminary transfers to Ridgefield, CT.

1980 Anniversary & Acquisitions: SSPX celebrates its 10th Anniversary; the acquisition of St. Vincent DePaul Parish in Kansas City, Mo; opening of Institut Universitaire St. Pie X.

1980 Seminarians: Econe sees the arrival of 9 seminarians from Argentina to finish their theology studies; Ridgefield, CT have 12 new candidates.

>   FR. MICHAEL GABRIELLI (CONT'D)
>   It is at this time that the
>   Archbishop realizes the SSPX order
>   needs many more priests to fulfill
>   the requests.
>   (MORE)

(CONTINUED)

MARCEL: The Right Hand of God
CONTINUED:

> **FR. MICHAEL GABRIELLI (CONT'D)**
> The Archbishop makes a statement that *"We are asked from everywhere in the world to form and send priests, As of todayI would need to have 150 or 200 extra priests to answer the requests of the faithful"*.
>
> **FR. WALTER JAEGER**
> So much for the statements that only a few people make great noise.
>
> **FR. MICHAEL GABRIELLI**
> Exactly, the world cried for the tradition and that was one of the main reasons Pope John Paul II decided to lift the restriction against the Latin Mass that his predecessor imposed years before.
>
> **FR. WALTER JAEGER**
> I heard that in the early 1980's the people of Mexico reached out for the Archbishop.
>
> **FR. MICHAEL GABRIELLI**
> Yes they did.

1981 Mexican Invasion: The visit of the Archbishop to a new Chapel (Jesus and Mary) in El Paso, Texas allowed many of the Mexican faithful to hear about the SSPX. The Archbishop decides to visit Mexico after years of being prohibited by the Mexican government and the people in Southern Mexico great him like a conquering hero. The exclaim "el hombre justo" - "The Just Man".

1981 Africa, South America & Australia: The Archbishop goes for a long missionary trip to South Africa and the to Argentina where on August 15th he lays the cornerstone of the seminary in La Reja (near Buenos Aires). That same year he travels to Australia to prepare the foundation of the first priory in Sydney.

1982 London Acquisition On March 1st, attributed to the prays of St. Joseph the Society buys its first Church in London with 300 faithful parishioners.

1982 Cardinal Ratzinger is appointed: Cardinal Joseph Ratzinger becomes the new Secretary of State under Pope John Paul II.

(CONTINUED)

MARCEL: The Right Hand of God
CONTINUED:

> FR. MICHAEL GABRIELLI (CONT'D)
> This is when the cracks start to form.

> FR. WALTER JAEGER
> In what way Father? With the Society?

> FR. MICHAEL GABRIELLI
> No with the Vatican II oppression. Cardinal Ratzinger asks for an interview with the Archbishop. They meet for a long time.

> FR. WALTER JAEGER
> What was the content of the meeting?

> FR. MICHAEL GABRIELLI
> Cardinal Ratzinger states that Rome wants the Society to say that even though they may have some reservations about it, the liturgical reform is good and that the Society just believe it is less good than the old liturgy.

> FR. WALTER JAEGER
> How did the Archbishop respond to that?

> FR. MICHAEL GABRIELLI
> He said: "*Now we believe the reform is evil, poisoned by ecumenism, and we refuse to accept it and we are obliged to advise all the faithful against it. God only knows how long the reformers will close their eyes to the destruction of the faith, of morals of institutions*"

> FR. WALTER JAEGER
> Sure that went over well with Cardinal Ratzinger and Rome.

> FR. MICHAEL GABRIELLI
> At that point the Archbishop didn't care. He was in it for the long fight. The good fight. The just fight.

(CONTINUED)

MARCEL: The Right Hand of God
CONTINUED:

1982 All Night Vigil: An all-night prayer vigil us held in Martigny, near Econe, inspired by Our Lady of Fatima's message asking for prayer and penance. 3,000 pilgrims attend and the Archbishop declares calmly and firmly: *"The 21st century will be Catholic or it will not be at all!"*

1982 New Vicar General: Fr. Franz Schmidberger is elected Vicar General with right of immediate succession as Superior General. The seminary course of studies is extended from 5 to 6 years. The Society have 60 new entries in Econe, Ridgefield, Zaitzkofen and Buenos Aires.

> FR. WALTER JAEGER
> By your fruits you shall no them?

> FR. MICHAEL GABRIELLI
> Exactly!

1983 Ratzinger Letter to the Archbishop: Cardinal Ratzinger writes the following to the Archbishop: *"The Pope acknowledges the devotion of Archbishop Lefebvre and his fundamental attachment to the Holy See, expressed for instance by the exclusion of members who do not recognize the authority of the Pope"*

> FR. WALTER JAEGER
> Why did Cardinal Ratzinger send this letter?

> FR. MICHAEL GABRIELLI
> Because many said that the Archbishop was a sedavacantist, you know *"did not believe the Pope had authority over the Church"* But the Archbishop made it very clear he would never support such individuals and even refused candidates into the seminary if they held these views.

1984 SSPX Status: The Society reaches 120 Priests, Econe has 120 Seminarians.

1985 Televised Praise of the Archbishop: A well deserved tribute is featured in a television broadcast for the work that the Archbishop achieved in Gabon, Africa.

1985 Petitions: Fr. Schmidberger presents Cardinal Ratzinger three large packages with petitions of 129,849 Traditional Catholics asking the Pope to solve the problem of tradition.

(CONTINUED)

MARCEL: The Right Hand of God
CONTINUED:

1985 Ireland and Germany Expansion: The Society acquires a new Church in Dublin for 700 faithful parishioners and 10 new Chapels are opened in Germany.

1985 - 80th Birthday: The Archbishop celebrates his 80th Birthday in Argentina.

1986 Pope Announces Meetings with SSPX: Cardinal Gagnon calls the Archbishop to Rome and announces that the Holy Father wants him to be associated to Cardinal Ratzinger in the Societies case.

1986 - Gabon: The Society founds a house in Gabon, Africa and the President invites the Archbishop to visit the country.

1986 - Armada: The Society Sisters found a novitiate at Armada, MI. The US headquarters of the Society moves from Dickenson, Texas to St. Louis, MO.

1987 SSPX Status: The Society has 205 Priests working in 23 countries and 263 young men filling the seminaries. In Ridgefield, CT, the arrival of 19 new seminarians.

1987 - Departing Catholics: Rome reports that 60 Million Catholics in South America have left the Catholic Church and joined the Protestant Church. The Archbishop writes a book to address this loss of Catholics. The book is titled "*They have Uncrowned Him*"

1987 Meeting with Ratzinger: On July 14th the Archbishop meets with Ratizinger regarding the naming of Bishops for SSPX.

>   FR. WALTER JAEGER
>   Is this what started the
>   excommunication of the Archbishop?
>
>   FR. MICHAEL GABRIELLI
>   Yes. The Archbishop new he did not
>   have many more years to live. He
>   was in his 80's and if a Bishop was
>   not made, the Society could no
>   longer ordain Priests and continue
>   with the traditional order that the
>   Society was founded on.
>
>   FR. WALTER JAEGER
>   What did the Archbishop request?

(CONTINUED)

MARCEL: The Right Hand of God
   CONTINUED:

>   FR. MICHAEL GABRIELLI
>   In their very first meeting the
>   Archbishop stated: *"Your Eminence,
>   for us Jesus Christ is everything;
>   he is the Church, he is the
>   priesthood, He is our apostolate,
>   He is the Catholic family, He is
>   the Catholic state. If you do not
>   name bishops to assure my
>   succession, my duty as an
>   Archbishop is to do it myself"*
>
>   FR. WALTER JAEGER
>   Was his concern that Rome was just
>   waiting for him to die and so goes
>   the Society?
>
>   FR. MICHAEL GABRIELLI
>   Of course! He was the thorn in
>   their Liberal side. After 20 years
>   of an unsuccessful dialogue with
>   Rome, everything seemed to indicate
>   that Rome was just waiting for the
>   death of the Archbishop to give the
>   final stroke against traditional
>   works. But in July of 1987 the
>   Society acquires a great Seminary.

1987 Dominican Novitiate House: In Winona, MN, where a magnificent building that belonged to the Dominican order, was purchased as the new seminary in the US. The seminarians move from Ridgefield, CT to Winona, MN.

1987 Cardinal Ratzinger makes Offer: Cardinal Ratzinger writes to the Archbishop offering a proposal for a solution which includes a possible visit to the Society.

1987 Pope Requests Visit to Society: Pope John Paul II asked Canadian Cardinal Edouard Gagnon, President of the Pontical Council for the Family, to make a month-long visit of the houses and chapels of the SSPX.

1988 - The Gagnon Report: On January 5, 1988, Cardinal Gagnon presents the Pope a 39 page report.

1988 - Archbishop Announces Consecration of Bishops: On February 2, 1988 the Archbishop announces before television camera's that he will consecrate 3 Bishops on June 30, 1988.

                                                    (CONTINUED)

CONTINUED:

> **FR. WALTER JAEGER**
> So this was the day of all days for the Society. This when the entire order is excommunicated, is it not?

> **FR. MICHAEL GABRIELLI**
> Well, there were many discussions that had gone on between Cardinal Ratzinger and the Archbishop.

> **FR. WALTER JAEGER**
> But didn't Cardinal Ratzinger do all in his power to try and stop Pope John Paul II from excommunicating the Archbishop and the Society?

> **FR. MICHAEL GABRIELLI**
> You must remember that Cardinal Ratzinger was a product of Vatican II. He truly believed in his heart as he still does today that there could be two liturgies and so although he was trying to do his best, he was constantly trying to get the Archbishop to recognize the Second Vatican Council doctrines and that was never possible to the Archbishop.

> **FR. WALTER JAEGER**
> But I thought Cardinal Ratzinger and the Pope agreed to allow the Archbishop to consecrate the Bishops.

> **FR. MICHAEL GABRIELLI**
> They did in words but not in actions. They kept trying to postpone the consecration of the bishops almost as if to use it as a tool of concession. The Archbishop had already taken on all the insults of the past in being suspended and the Mass being refused and then reinstated. He knew that there was no good reason to stop him from consecrating bishops anymore than refusing him to train traditional priests or say the traditional Mass.
> (MORE)

MARCEL: The Right Hand of God
CONTINUED:

FR. MICHAEL GABRIELLI (CONT'D)
In short, he had enough and he was more concerned with his own death being a final straw. So out of necessity he continued as planned the consecration of the 4 Bishops.

FR. WALTER JAEGER
Did the Archbishop every have remorse over how he handled the consecration of the bishops? Did he ever feel he could have handled it differently with Cardinal Ratzinger and Pope John Paul II?

FR MARCEL LEFEBVRE
No, as a matter of fact he was asked that questions and responded: "*Absolutely not. Everything was truly providential and almost miraculous. I was pressured from many sides for a long time and I could have ordained bishops 3 or 4 years earlier; it would even have been reasonable for me to do so, but I believe that God wanted things to develop slowly so that we could show to Rome and to history that we have done all we could to finally obtain the authorization to have traditional bishops. The faithful will be more and more numerous and they will open their eyes to see finally what is the truth in this affair.*"

FR. WALTER JAEGER
So they even removed his name from the Pontifical Directory?

FR. MICHAEL GABRIELLI
Yes they did but the Archbishop responded to that by saying: "*I know my name has been removed from the Pontifical Directory, but I hope that it is not disappeared from the Directory of our dear Lord and this is what really matters.*"

FR. WALTER JAEGER
So is that the 100 years you were referring to Father?

(CONTINUED)

MARCEL: The Right Hand of God
CONTINUED:

> **FR. MICHAEL GABRIELLI**
> Yes and the Archbishop proved to be the truest of all soldiers. When the devil had reared his ugly head during the 1960's and 1970's and even had the Church in his grips, the Archbishop stood fast and firm as he promised Pope Pius XII he would.
>
> **FR. WALTER JAEGER**
> The Archbishop didn't live much longer did her Father?
>
> **FR. MICHAEL GABRIELLI**
> No. He died on March 25, 1991. According to the ancient martyrologies this was also the date of our Lords death as well. How appropriate.
>
> **FR. WALTER JAEGER**
> Does he have anything written on his tombstone?
>
> **FR. MICHAEL GABRIELLI**
> Yes, very simply he had written *"Tradidi quod et accepi"* which means *"I have transmitted what I have received"*.
>
> **FR. WALTER JAEGER**
> So even since his death the Society continues to grow and flourish throughout the world.
>
> **FR MARCEL LEFEBVRE**
> Yes and do you know why? Because it was never about the Archbishop. It was always about Our Lord. He is the Church. And as the Archbishop repeated constantly *"By our fruits they shall know us"*.
>
> **FR. WALTER JAEGER**
> So would you say the once Cardinal Ratzinger our Pope now in Benedict XVI had regrets for his conduct and that is why he fully reinstated the Traditional Latin Mass?

(CONTINUED)

MARCEL: The Right Hand of God
CONTINUED:

> FR MARCEL LEFEBVRE
> I would like to believe so. I truly feel our Holy Father looks at the fruits of Vatican II and then the fruits of Tradition and realized he and all the other Bishops and Cardinals before him were no better than King Henry VIII. They torture St. Thomas Moore all over again. Only this man was able to stop the Protestant Reformation in its tracks. He was truly the right hand of God.

> FR. WALTER JAEGER
> So Father, I was born into Vatican II like many others. We never had the formation you had. We never knew anything but the New Mass. Why did you, after going through formation with the Holy Ghost Fathers and having such a great Superior General and role model like Archbishop Lefebvre go along with these changes. Why did you not take a stand like the Archbishop? Why did you stand by and watch when he was being persecuted and do nothing?

> FR. MICHAEL GABRIELLI
> Why didn't I take a stand? Why didn't I follow in the Archbishops foot steps?

> FR. WALTER JAEGER
> Yes!

> FR. MICHAEL GABRIELLI
> Because like many others I just assumed things would eventually turn out for the better.

> FR. WALTER JAEGER
> So you could not tell that the new way was not bearing good fruit?

> FR. MICHAEL GABRIELLI
> I knew. Yes I knew. I saw the destruction everywhere.
> (MORE)

(CONTINUED)

MARCEL: The Right Hand of God
CONTINUED:

> FR. MICHAEL GABRIELLI (CONT'D)
> In the Church, in the families, in the society and everywhere in the world.

> FR. WALTER JAEGER
> So when did you know the fruits were bad. What year did it hit you?

> FR. MICHAEL GABRIELLI
> By 1979 I already knew what the new order was all about. It was bad!

> FR. WALTER JAEGER
> And so you let another 20 years go by? Why?

> FR. MICHAEL GABRIELLI
> Because unlike Archbishop Lefebvre

Long pause as he looks around in a state of confusion and self judgement.

> FR. MICHAEL GABRIELLI (CONT'D)
> Because unlike Archbishop Lefebvre, me and many millions like me ....
> WERE COWARDS!

The final scene in the movie will be the press coverage of the Pope lifting the excommunications in January, 2009 and a loud scream from the devil as if his time (100 YEARS) has ended.

The following quote appears on the screen "….. **at the present time there is a remnant left selected out of grace and truth**"

- **Romans 11:05**

Printed in Poland
by Amazon Fulfillment
Poland Sp. z o.o., Wrocław